THE COMPANION.

After-Dinner Table-Talk.

The Revd Sydney Smith.

THE COMPANION.

After-Dinner Table-Talk.

By Chetwood Evelyn, Esq.

"This is the motley-minded gentleman."
As You Like It.

NEW YORK:

GEORGE P. PUTNAM, 155 BROADWAY.

1850.

STEREOTYPED BY
BILLIN & BRO'S,
10 North William-street, New York.

TO YOU,

My dear Cousin Eliza,

THIS BOOK

IS MOST AFFECTIONATELY DEDICATED.

CHETWOOD EVELYN.

" SCARAMOUCH, THE FIRST FAMOUS ITALIAN COMEDIAN, BEING AT PARIS AND IN GREAT WANT, BETHOUGHT HIMSELF OF CONSTANTLY PLYING NEAR THE DOOR OF A NOTED PERFUMER IN THAT CITY, AND WHEN ANY ONE CAME OUT WHO HAD BEEN BUYING SNUFF, NEVER FAILED TO DESIRE A TASTE OF THEM; WHEN HE HAD BY THIS MEANS GOT TOGETHER A QUANTITY MADE UP OF SEVERAL DIFFERENT SORTS, HE SOLD IT AGAIN AT A LOWER RATE TO THE SAME PERFUMER, WHO, FINDING OUT THE TRICK, CALLED IT 'TABAC DE MILLE FLEURS,' OR 'SNUFF OF A THOUSAND FLOWERS.' BY THIS MEANS HE GOT A VERY COMFORTABLE SUBSISTENCE, UNTIL MAKING TOO MUCH HASTE TO BE RICH, HE ONE DAY TOOK SUCH AN UNREASONABLE PINCH——"

Spectator, No. 283.

AFTER-DINNER TABLE-TALK.

WIT AND PROFESSED WITS.

I WISH, after all I have said about wit and humour, I could satisfy myself of their good effects upon the character and disposition; but I am convinced the probable tendency of both is, to corrupt the understanding and the heart. I am not speaking of wit where it is kept down by more serious qualities of mind, and thrown into the background of the picture; but where it stands out boldly and emphatically, and is evidently the master quality in any particular mind. Professed wits, though they are generally courted for the amusement they afford, are seldom respected for the qualities they possess. The habit of seeing things in a witty point of view increases, and makes incursions from its own proper regions upon principles and opinions which are ever held sacred by the wise and good. A witty man is a dramatic performer: in process of time, he can no more exist without applause than he can without air; if his audience be small, or if they are inattentive, or if a new wit defrauds him of any portion of his admiration, it is all over with him, — he sickens, and is extinguished. The applauses of the theatre on which he performs are so essential to him, that he must obtain them at the expense of decency, friendship, and good feeling. It must always be *probable*, too, that a *mere* wit is a person of light and frivolous understanding. His business is not to discover relations of ideas that are *useful*, and have a real influence upon life, but to discover the more trifling relations which are only amusing; he never looks at things with the naked eye of common-sense, but is always gazing at the world through a Claude Lorraine glass, discovering a thousand appearances which are created only by the instrument of inspection, and covering every object with facetious and unnatural colours. In short, the character of a *mere* wit it is impossible to consider as very amiable, very respectable, or very safe. So far the world, in judging of wit where it has swallowed up all other qualifications, judge aright; but I doubt if they are sufficiently indulgent to this faculty where it exists in a lesser degree, and as one out of many other ingredients of the understanding. There is an association in men's minds between dullness and wisdom, amusement and folly, which has a very powerful influence in decision upon character, and is not overcome without considerable difficulty. The reason is, that the *outward* sign of a dull man and a wise man are the same, and so are the outward signs of a frivolous man and a witty man; and we are not to expect that the majority will be disposed to look to much *more* than the outward sign. I believe the fact to be, that wit is very seldom the *only* eminent quality which resides in the mind of any man; it is commonly accompanied with many other talents of every description, and ought to be considered as a strong evidence of a fertile and superior understanding. Almost all the great poets, orators, and statesmen of all times, have been witty. Cæsar, Alexander, Aristotle, Descartes, and Lord Bacon, were witty men; so was Cicero, Shakspeare, Demosthenes, Boileau, Pope, Dryden, Fontenelle, Jonson, Waller, Cowley, Solon, Socrates, Dr. Johnson, and almost every man who has made a distinguished figure in the House of Commons. I have talked of the *danger* of wit; I do not mean by that to enter into common-place declamation against faculties because they *are* dangerous; wit is dangerous, eloquence is dangerous, a talent for observation is dangerous, *every* thing is dangerous that has efficacy and vigour for its characteristics; nothing is safe but mediocrity. The business is, in conducting the understanding well, to risk something; to aim at uniting things that are commonly incompatible. The meaning of an extraordinary man is, that he is *eight* men, not one man; that he has as much wit as if he had no sense, and as much sense as if he had no wit; that his conduct is as judicious as if he were the

dullest of human beings, and his imagination as brilliant as if he were irretrievably ruined. But when wit is combined with sense and information; when it is softened by benevolence, and restrained by strong principle; when it is in the hands of a man who can use it and despise it, who can be witty and something much *better* than witty, who loves honour, justice, decency, good-nature, morality, and religion, ten thousand times better than wit; wit is *then* a beautiful and delightful part of our nature. There is no more interesting spectacle than to see the effects of wit upon the different characters of men; than to observe it expanding caution, relaxing dignity, unfreezing coldness, teaching age, and care, and pain, to smile, extorting reluctant gleams of pleasure from melancholy, and charming even the pangs of grief. It is pleasant to observe how it penetrates through the coldness and awkwardness of society, gradually bringing men nearer together, and, like the combined force of wine and oil, giving every man a glad heart and a shining countenance. Genuine and innocent wit like this, is surely the *flavour of the mind!* Man could direct his ways by plain reason, and support his life by tasteless food; but God has given us wit, and flavour, and brightness, and laughter, and perfumes, to enliven the days of man's pilgrimage, and to "charm his pained steps over the burning marle."
—*Sydney Smith.*

RAILLERY.

Raillery is the finest part of conversation; but, as it is our usual custom to counterfeit and adulterate whatever is too dear for us, so we have done with this, and turn it all into what is generally called repartee, or being smart; just as when an expensive fashion comes up, those who are not able to reach it, content themselves with some paltry imitation. It now passes for raillery to run a man down in discourse, to put him out of countenance, and make him ridiculous; sometimes to expose the defects of his person or understanding; on all which occasions, he is obliged not to be angry, to avoid the imputation of not being able to take a jest. It is admirable to observe one who is dexterous at this art, singling out a weak adversary, getting the laugh on his side, and then carrying all before him. The French, from whence we borrow the word, have a quite different idea of the thing, and so had we in the politer age of our fathers. Raillery, was to say something that at first appeared a reproach or reflection, but, by some turn of wit unexpected and surprising, ended always in a compliment, and to the advantage of the person it was addressed to. And surely one of the best rules in conversation is, never to say a thing which any of the company can reasonably wish we had rather left unsaid: nor can there any thing be well more contrary to the ends for which people meet together, than to part unsatisfied with each other or themselves.—*Swift.*

In exemplification of this, we may give an anec

dote of the duke of Buckingham. "My lord," said he to the earl of Orrery, "you will certainly be damned." "How, my lord?" said the earl, with some warmth. "Nay, nay, there is no help for it," answered the duke, "for it is positively said, 'Cursed is he of whom all men speak well.'"

This is taking a man by surprise, and being welcome when you have surprised him. The person flattered receives you into his closet at once; and the sudden change of his heart, from the expectation of an ill-wisher, to find you his friend, makes you in his full favour in a moment, more so than if you had paid him the finest compliment. The spirits that were raised so suddenly against you, are as suddenly raised for you.

PASSING ONE'S TIME.

There is no saying shocks me so much as that which I hear very often, "that a man does not know how to pass his time." It would have been but ill-spoken by Methusalah in the nine hundred and sixty-ninth year of his life.—*Cowley.*

WITTY SIMILE.

Sir Harry Hargrave's mind is full of the most obsolete errors; a very Monmouth-street of threadbare prejudices: if a truth gleam for a moment upon him, it discomposes all his habit of thought, like a stray sunbeam on a cave full of bats.—*Bulwer.*

TRUTH.

When a man has no design but to speak plain truth, he may say a great deal in a very narrow compass.—*Steele.*

ANGLERS.

Old Walton, in his "Complete Angler," after having given some choice directions how to dress a pike, observes that "this dish of meat is too good for any but anglers, or very honest men."

LIBRARIES

Are as the shrines where all the relics of saints, full of true virtue, and that without delusion and imposture, are preserved and reposed.—*Bacon.*

AFFECTATION OF GRANDEUR.

Senecio was a man of a turbid and confused wit, who could not endure to speak any but mighty words and sentences, till this humour grew at last into so notorious a habit, or rather disease, as became the sport of the whole town; he would have no servants but huge, massy fellows; no plate or household stuff but thrice as big as the fashion; you may believe, (for I speak it without raillery,) his extravagancy came at last into a madness, that he would not put on a pair of shoes, each of which was not big enough for both his feet; he would eat nothing but what was great, nor touch any fruit but horse-plums and pound-pears.—*Seneca.*

LOVE OF LITTLENESS.

I confess, I love littleness almost in all things. A little convenient estate, a little cheerful house, a little company, and a very little feast, and, if I were ever to fall in love again, (which is a great passion, and therefore I hope I have done with it,) it would be, I think, with prettiness, rather than with majestical beauty.—*Cowley.*

"THE GREAT VULGAR."

Successful poets have a great authority over the language of their country. Cowley's happy expression of "the great vulgar," is become a part of the English phraseology.—*Hurd.*

THE STRAWBERRY.

Dr. Butler said of strawberries, "Doubtless God could have made a better berry, but doubtless God never did."

A HABITUAL BORE.

Lord Chesterton we have often met with, and suffered a good deal from his lordship: a heavy, pompous, meddling peer, occupying a great share of the conversation—saying things in ten words which required only two, and evidently convinced that he is making a great impression; a large man with a large head, and a very landed manner, knowing enough to torment his fellow-creatures, not to instruct them, the ridicule of young ladies, and the natural butt and target of wit. It is easy to talk of carnivorous animals and beasts of prey, but does such a man, who lays waste a whole civilized party of beings by prosing, reflect upon the joy he spoils, and the misery he creates, in the course of his life? and that any one who listens to him through politeness, would prefer toothache or earache to his conversation? Does he consider the extreme uneasiness which ensues when the company have discovered a man to be an extremely absurd person, at the same time that it is absolutely impossible to convey, by words or manner the most distant suspicion of the discovery? And, then, who punishes this bore? What sessions or what assizes for him? What bill is found against him? Who indicts him? When the judges have gone their vernal and autumnal rounds, the sheepstealer disappears—the swindler gets ready for the Bay—the solid parts of the murderer are preserved in anatomical collections. But after twenty years of crime, the bore is discovered in the same house, in the same attitude, eating the same soup—untried—unpunished—undissected.—*Sydney Smith.*

DIFFICULT QUESTIONS.

When Coleridge in 1799, went to Germany, he left word to Lamb, that if he wished any information on any subject he might apply to him, (*i. e.* by letter,) so Lamb sends him the following abstruse propositions, to which, however, Coleridge did not "deign an answer."

Whether God loves a lying angel better than a true man?

Whether the archangel Uriel *could* knowingly affirm an untruth, and whether, if he *could*, he *would?*

Whether the higher order of seraphim illuminati ever *sneer?*

Whether an immortal and amenable soul may not come *to be damned at last*, and the man never suspect it beforehand?

GENIUS AND COMMON UNDERSTANDING.

There is a lower kind of discretion and regularity, which seldom fails of raising men to the highest stations, in the court, the church, and the law. It must be so: for Providence, which designed the world should be governed by many heads, made it a business within the reach of common understandings; while one great genius is hardly found in ten millions. Did you never observe one of your clerks cutting his paper with a blunt ivory knife? did you ever know the knife to fail going the true way? whereas if he had used a razor or penknife, he had odds against him of spoiling a whole sheet.—*Swift to Bolingbroke.*

STUPID STORIES.

"A stupid story," says Walpole, "or idea, will sometimes make one laugh more than wit."

LOSING TIME.

One night when Matthews was going to the theatre at Edinburgh, and was almost too late, he took a coach, and ordered the coachman to drive to the theatre. In going up the hill, the horses being tired, the coach made no progress, upon which Matthews remonstrated, saying, that he should be too late, he should lose his time. The coachman coolly said, "Your honour should reflact that I'm losing time as weel's yersel'."

DELICATE PRAISE.

When Sir Matthew Hale was made chief-justice, his commission was brought to him by Lord Clarendon, who told him, that, "if the king could have found out an honester and a fitter man for that employment, he would not have advanced him to it."

A HAPPY CHARACTER.

He is a most lively, good-humoured, and pleasant man, who bears the ills of life as if they were blessings, and seems to take the rough and smooth with an equal countenance. This sort of unbended philosophy is the best gift that nature can bestow on her children; it lightens the burden of care, and turns every fable, and ghastly hue of memory, to bright and splendid colours. There is no one I enjoy so much as I do him; a cap and bells is a crown to him; a tune upon a flageolet is a concert;

if the sun shines, he sports himself in its beams; if the storm comes he skips gayly along, and when he is wet to the skin it only serves to make out a pleasant story, while he is drying himself at the fire. If you are dull after dinner, he will get him up, and rehearse half a dozen scenes out of a play, and do it well, and be as pleased with his performance as you can be. With all these companionable talents, he is neither forward, noisy, or impertinent; but on the contrary very conversable; and possesses as pleasant a kind of good-breeding as any one.—*Lord Lyttleton's Letters.*

HERALDRY *v.* AGRICULTURE.

We may talk what we please of lilies, and lions rampant, and spread eagles, in fields of *d'or* or *d'argent*, but if heraldry were guided by reason, a plough in a field arable would be the most noble and ancient arms.—*Cowley.*

MOVING.

What a dislocation of comfort is implied in that word moving! Such a heap of little, nasty things, after you think all is got into the cart; old dredging boxes, worn-out brushes, gallipots, vials, things that it is impossible the most necessitous person can ever want, but which the women, who preside on these occasions, will not leave behind, if it was to save your soul: they'd keep the cart ten minutes, to stow in dirty pipes and broken matches, to show their economy. Then you can find nothing you want for many days after you get into your new lodgings. You must comb your hair with your fingers, wash your hands without soap, go about in dirty gaiters.—*Charles Lamb.*

MONK LEWIS'S TRAGEDY OF ALFONSO.

This tragedy delights in explosions. Alfonso's empire is destroyed by a blast of gunpowder, and restored by a clap of thunder. After the death of Cæsario, and a short exhortation to that purpose by Orsino, all the conspirators fall down in a thunder-clap, ask pardon of the king, and are forgiven. This mixture of physical and moral power is beautiful! How interesting a water-spout would appear among Mr. Lewis's kings and queens. We anxiously look forward, in his next tragedy, to a fall of snow, three or four feet deep, or expect that a plot shall gradually unfold itself by means of a general thaw.—*Sydney Smith.*

ENGLISH CONVERSATION.

Hesitating, Humming, and Drawling, are the three graces of English Conversation. We are at dinner—a gentleman, "a man about town," is informing us of a misfortune that has befallen his friend. "No—I assure you—now—err—err—that—err—it was the most shocking accident possible—err—poor Chester was riding in the park—err—you know that grey—err, (substantive dropped, hand a little flourished instead,)—of his—splendid creature!—err—well, sir, and by Jove—err—the—err—(no substantive, flourish again,) took fright, and—e—err—" Here the gentleman throws up his chin and eyes, sinks back exhausted into his chair, and after a pause adds—"Well, they took him into the shop—there—you know—with the mahogany sashes—just by the park—err—and—err—man there—set his—what d'ye call it—collar-bone; *but* he was—err—ter—ri—bly—terribly—" (a full stop.) The gentleman shakes his head, and the sentence is suspended to eternity.

Another gentleman takes up the wondrous tale, logically: "Ah! shocking, shocking—*but* poor Chester was a very agreeable—err—" (full stop.)

"Oh! devilish gentlemanlike fellow!—quite shocking!—quite—did you go into the—err—to-day?"

"No, indeed; the day was so un—may I take some wine with you?"

But, perhaps, the genius of our conversation is most shown in the art of explaining.

"Were you in the house last night?"

"Yes—err—Sir Robert Peel made a splendid speech!"

"Ah! how did he justify his vote? I've not seen the papers."

"Oh, I can tell exactly—ehem—he said—you see—that he disliked the ministers, and so forth! you understand—but that—err—in these times, and so forth—and with this river of blood—oh! he was very fine *there!*—you must read it—well, sir; and then he was very good against O'Connell, capital—and all this agitation *going on*—and murder, and so forth—and then, sir, he told a capital story, about a man and his wife being murdered; and putting a child in a fireplace—you see—I forget now, but it was capital: and then he wound up with—a—with—a—in his usual way, in short, oh! he quite justified himself—you understand—in short, you see, he could not do otherwise."

Caricatured as this may seem, I assure you that it is to the life: the explainer, too, is reckoned a very sensible man; and the listener saw nothing inclusive in the elucidation.—*England and the English. Bulwer.*

MR. THOMAS HILL.

Mr. Hill died a year or two ago—aged, we believe, not more than eighty-three, though Hook and all his friends affected to consider him as quite a Methusalah. James Smith said once, that it was impossible to discover his age, for the parish register had been burned in the fire of London—but Hook capped this: "Pooh, pooh! he's one of the Little Hills that are spoken of as skipping in the Psalms." As a mere octogenarian he was wonderful enough, no human being would, from his appearance, gait, or habits, have guessed him to be sixty. Till within three months of his death he rose at five usually, and brought the materials of his breakfast home with him to the Adelphi, from a walk to Billingsgate; and at dinner he would eat and drink like an adjutant of five-and-twenty. One secret was, that a banyan day uniformly followed a festivity. He then nursed himself most carefully on tea and dry toast, tasted neither meat nor wine, and went to bed by eight o'clock. But perhaps the grand secret was, the easy, imperturbable serenity of his temper. He had been kind and generous in the day of his wealth, and although his evening was comparatively poor, his cheerful heart kept its even beat.—*Quarterly Review.*

TITLES OF BOOKS.

There is a kind of physiognomy in the titles of books no less than in the faces of men, by which a skillful observer will as well know what to expect from the one as the other.—*Butler.*

THE PLEASURES OF LONDON.

Streets, streets, streets, markets, theatres, churches, Covent Gardens; shops sparkling with pretty faces of industrious milliners; neat seamstresses; ladies cheapening; gentlemen behind counters lying; authors in the streets with spectacles, (you may know them by their gait;) lamps lighted at night; pastrycook and silversmiths' shops; beautiful quakers of Pentonville; noise of coaches; drowsy cry of mechanic watchmen by night, with bucks reeling home drunk; if you happen to wake at midnight, cries of fire and stop thief; Inns of Court, with their learned air, and stalls and butteries just like Cambridge colleges; old bookstalls, "Jeremy Taylors," "Burtons on Melancholy," and "Religio Medicis," on every stall. These are thy pleasures, O London!—*Lamb.*

GENTLEMAN'S MAGAZINE.

That great lumber-room wherein small ware of all kinds has been laid up higgledy-piggledy, by half-pennyworths or farthingworths at a time, for four-score years, till, like broken glass, rags, or rubbish, it has acquired value by mere accumulation.—*The Doctor.*

ALEXANDER HAMILTON.

The discerning eye of Washington immediately called him to that post which was infinitely the most important in the administration of the new system. Hamilton was made secretary of the treasury; and how he fulfilled the duties of such a place, at such a time, the whole country saw with admiration. He smote the rock of the national resources, and the abundant stream of revenue gushed forth. He touched the dead corpse of the public credit, and it sprang upon its feet.—*Daniel Webster.*

GEORGE SELWYN'S BON-MOTS.

We shall here quote some of the best of Selwyn's witticisms and pleasantries, and prefer rather throwing them all together, than to scatter them here and there about the book; as it enables us to see better at a glance the character and style of Selwyn's wit.

When a subscription was proposed for Fox, and some one was observing that it required some delicacy, and wondering how Fox would take it. "Take it? why, quarterly to be sure."

When one of the Foley family crossed the Channel to avoid his creditors—"It is a *passover* that will not be much relished by the Jews."

When Fox was boasting of having prevailed on the French court to give up the gum trade—"As you have permitted the French to draw your teeth, they would be fools, indeed, to quarrel with you about your gums."

At the trial of the rebel lords, seeing Bethel's sharp visage looking wistfully at the prisoners, he said: "What a shame it is to turn her face to the prisoners until they are condemned."

Some women were scolding Selwyn for going to see the execution, and asked him how he could be such a barbarian to see the head cut off? "Nay," replied he, "if that was such a crime, I am sure I have made amends; for I went to see it sewed on again."

One night at White's, observing the Postmaster-general, Sir Everard Fawkener, losing a large sum of money at piquet, pointing to the successful player, he remarked—"See how he's robbing the mail!"

On another occasion, in 1756, observing Mr. Ponsonby, the Speaker of the Irish House of Commons, tossing about bank-bills at a hazard-table at New market—"Look how easily the Speaker passes the money-bills."

The beautiful Lady Coventry was exhibiting to him a splendid new dress, covered with large silver spangles the size of a shilling, and inquired of him whether he admired her taste—"Why," said he, "you will be *change for a guinea.*"

At the sale of the effects of the minister, Mr. Pelham, Selwyn, pointing to a silver dinner-service, observed—"Lord, how many toads have been eaten off those plates!"

A namesake of Charles Fox having been hung at Tyburn, Fox inquired of Selwyn whether he had attended the execution—"No, I make a point of never frequenting *rehearsals.*"

A fellow-passenger in a coach, imagining from his appearance that he was suffering from illness, kept wearying him with good-natured inquiries as to the state of his health. At length to the repeated question of "How are you now, sir?" Selwyn replied—"Very well, I thank you; and I mean to continue so for the rest of the journey."

He was one day walking with Lord Pembroke, when they were besieged by a number of young chimney-sweepers, who kept plaguing them for money; at length Selwyn made them a low bow—"I have often," he said, "heard of the sovereignty of the people; I suppose your highnesses are in court mourning."—*Edinburgh Review.*

AMERICAN ICE.

Sydney Smith, in London, was shown a lump of American ice, upon which he remarked, "that he was glad to see any thing solvent come from America."

PLEASANT TIMES.

No arts, no letters, no society, and which is worst of all, continual fear and danger of violent death; and the life of man, solitary, poor, nasty, brutish, and short.—*Hobbes.*

MECHANICAL DUTY.

Schiller used to say, that he found the great happiness of life, after all, to consist in the discharge of some mechanical duty.

CURRAN.

I caught the first glimpse of the little man through the vista of his garden. There he was—on a third time afterward, I saw him in a dress which you would imagine he had borrowed from his tipstaff—his hands on his sides; his under lip protruded; his face almost parallel with the horizon; and the important step and eternal attitude only varied by the pause during which his eye glanced from his guest to his watch, and from his watch reproachfully to his dining-room: it was an invariable peculiarity—one second after four o'clock, and he would not wait for the viceroy. The moment he perceived me, he took me by the hand, said he would not have any one introduce me; and with a manner which I often thought was *charmed*, he at once banished every apprehension, and completely familiarized me at the priory. I had often seen Curran—often heard him—often read him; but no man ever knew any thing about him, who did not see him at his own table, with the few whom he selected. He was a little convivial deity; he soared in every region, and was at home in all—he touched every thing, and seemed as if he had created it; he mastered the human heart, with the same ease that he did his violin. You wept, and you laughed, and you wondered; and the wonderful creature who made you do all at will, never let it appear that he was more than your equal, and was quite willing, if you chose, to become your auditor. It is said of Swift that his rule was to allow a minute's pause after he had concluded, and then, if no person took up the conversation, to recommence himself. Curran had no conversational rule whatever: he spoke from impulse, and he had the art so to draw you into a participation, that, though you felt an inferiority it was quite a contented one. Indeed nothing could excel the urbanity of his demeanour. At the time I speak of he was turned sixty, yet he was as playful as a child. The extremes of youth and age were met in him: he had the experience of the one, and the simplicity of the other.—*Philips's Recollections of Curran.*

ACTION.

Indolence is a delightful but distressing state; we must be doing something to be happy. Action is no less necessary than thought to the instinctive tendencies of the human frame.—*Hazlitt.*

"EVERY MAN'S HOUSE HIS CASTLE."

The following is Lord Chatham's brilliant illustration of the celebrated maxim in English law, that every man's house is his castle: "The poorest man may in his cottage bid defiance to all the forces of the crown. It may be frail; its roof may shake; the wind may blow through it; the storm may enter, the rain may enter—but the king of England cannot enter! all his forces dare not cross the threshold of the ruined tenement!"

ATTERBURY'S WIT.

Atterbury, the celebrated bishop of Rochester, the friend of the tory statesmen in the time of Queen Anne, happened to say in the House of Lords, while speaking on a certain bill then under discussion, that he had prophesied last winter this bill would be attempted in the present session, and he now was sorry to find he had proved a true prophet. Lord Coningsby, who spoke after the bishop, and always spoke in a passion, desired the house to remark that one of the right-reverend had set himself forth as a prophet; but, for his part, he did not know what prophet to liken him to, unless to that furious prophet Balaam, who was reproved by his own ass. Atterbury, in reply, with great wit and calmness exposed this rude attack, concluding thus: "Since the noble lord has discovered in our manners such a similitude, I am well content to be compared to the prophet Balaam; but, my lords, I am at a loss how to make out the other part of the parallel: I am sure that I have been reproved by nobody but his lordship!"

CURIOUS REMARK ON VANITY.

Franklin says: "Most people dislike vanity in others, whatever share they have of it themselves; but I give it fair quarter wherever I meet with it, being persuaded that it is often productive of good to the possessor, and to others who are within his sphere of action; and therefore, in many cases, it would not be altogether absurd if a man were to thank God for his *vanity*, among the other comforts of life."

HAPPY EPITHET.

Lord Erskine, speaking of animals, and hesitating to call them brutes, hit upon a happy phrase—the mute creation.

BAD TRANSLATORS.

It was the remark of Madame La Fayette, that a bad translator was like an ignorant footman, whose blundering messages disgraced his master by the awkwardness of the delivery, and frequently turned compliment into abuse, and politeness into rusticity.

BORES.

It is to be hoped that, with all the modern improvements, a mode will be discovered of getting rid of bores; for it is too bad that a poor wretch can be punished for stealing your pocket-handkerchief or gloves, and that no punishment can be inflicted on those who steal your time, and with it your temper and patience, as well as the bright thoughts that might have entered into your mind, (like the Irishman who lost the fortune before he had got it,) but were frightened away by the bore.—*Byron.*

SIR PHILIP FRANCIS.

A person having upon one occasion got Sir Philip Francis into a corner, and innocently mistaking his agitations and gestures for extreme interest in the narrative which he was administering to his patient, was somewhat confounded, when the latter, seizing him by the collar, exclaimed with an oath, that "Human nature could endure no more."

In all this, there was a consistency and uniformity that was extremely racy and amusing. He is not now present to cry out, "What does that mean, sir? what would you be at? No gibberish!" and therefore it may be observed that there was something exceedingly *piquant* in his character.

He was wont to say that he had nearly survived the good manly words of assent and denial, the *yes* and *no* of our ancestors, and could now hear nothing but "unquestionably," "certainly," "undeniably," or "by no means," and "I rather think not;" forms of speech to which he gave the most odious and contemptuous names, as effeminate and emasculated, and would turn into ridicule, by caricaturing the pronunciation of the words. Thus he would drawl out "unquestionably", in a faint childish tone, and then say, "Gracious God! does he mean *yes?* Then, why not say so at once, like a man?" As for the sliplsop of some fluent talkers in society, who exclaim that they are "*so* delighted," or "*so* shocked," and speak of things being pleasing or hateful "to a degree;" he would bear down upon them without mercy, and roar out, "To *what* degree? Your word means any thing, and every thing, and nothing."—*Brougham.*

POPE'S COMPLIMENTS.

Nothing ever exceeded Pope's compliments, in delicacy or elegance. Charles Lamb said they were the finest ever paid by the wit of man; that each of them is worth an estate for life.

What can be finer, or more artfully constructed, than that to Lord Conbury:

> "Would ye be blessed? despise low joys, low gains;
> Disdain whatever Conbury disdains;
> Be virtuous, and be happy for your pains."

And that masterly one to Lord Mansfield:

> "Conspicuous scene! another yet is nigh,
> (More silent far,) where kings and poets lie;
> Where Murray, (long enough his country's pride,)
> Shall be no more than Tully or than Hyde."

And with what a fine turn of indignant flattery, he addresses Lord Bolingbroke:

> "Why rail they then, if but one wreath of mine,
> Oh! all accomplished St. John! deck thy shrine?"

Discoursing of the "ruling passion," he says to Lord Cobham:

> "And you, brave Cobham! to the latest breath,
> Shall feel your ruling passion strong in death;
> Such in those moments, as in all the past,
> 'Oh! save my country, Heaven!' shall be your last."

Speaking of his grotto, (one of Pope's miserable affectations), he takes occasion to pay two very pretty compliments to Bolingbroke and Lord Peterborough.

> "There my retreat the best companions grace,
> Chiefs out of war, and statesmen out of place:
> There St. John mingles with my friendly bowl,
> The feast of reason and the flow of soul:
> And he, whose lightning pierc'd th' Iberian lines,
> Now forms my quincunx, and now ranks my vines;
> Or tames the genius of the stubborn plain,
> Almost as *quickly* as he conquered Spain.

Can there be any doubt, after reading these, whether Pope was a great poet or not?

INTELLECT IN TALL MEN.

Ofttimes such who are built four stories high, are observed to have very little in their cockloft.—*Fuller.*

WHITEFIELD.

Somebody inquired of Lady Townsend, whether it were true that Whitefield had *recanted:* "No," said she, "he has only *canted.*"

ASTONISHING PERSONS.

A man that astonishes at first, soon makes people impatient if he does not continue in the same andante key.—*Walpole.*

ORIGINALITY.

To mind the inside of a book is to entertain one's-self with the forced product of another man's brain. Now, I think, a man of quality and breeding may be much amused by the natural sprouts of his own.—*The Relapse.*

NOTHING TO DO.

Positively, the best thing a man can have to do is nothing, and, *next to that,* perhaps, good works.—*Lamb.*

MIND AND BODY.

Old Sir James Herring was remonstrated with for not rising earlier—"I can make up my mind to it," said he, "but cannot make up my body."

HOLY BULLIES.

How true it is of too many preachers, that which Sydney Smith says of Dr. Rennel, "that he is too apt to put on the appearance of a holy bully, as if he could carry his point against infidelity, by big words and strong abuse, and kick and cuff men into Christians."

ANECDOTE OF POPE, THE ACTOR.

Pope, the actor, well known for his devotion to the culinary art, received an invitation to dinner, accompanied by an apology for the simplicity of the intended fare—a small turbot and a boiled edge-bone of beef. "The very thing of all others that I like," exclaimed Pope; "I will come with the greatest pleasure." And come he did, and eat he did, till he could literally eat no longer; when the word was given, and a haunch of venison was brought in, fit to be made the subject of a new poetical epistle—

> "For finer or fatter,
> Never ranged in a forest, or smoked in a platter,
> The haunch was a picture for painters to study,
> The fat was so white, and the lean was so ruddy."

Poor Pope divined at a glance the nature of the trap that had been laid for him, but he was fairly caught, and after a puny effort at trifling with a slice of fat, he laid down his knife and fork, and gave way to a hysterical burst of tears, exclaiming—"a friend of twenty years' standing, and to be served in this manner."—*Quarterly Review.*

CURIOSITY.

Curiosity is a kernel of the forbidden fruit, which still sticketh in the throat of a natural man, sometimes to the danger of his choking.—*Fuller.*

WANT OF A PURSUIT.

A man without a predominant inclination is not likely to be either useful or happy. He who is every thing is nothing.—*Sharp.*

BRANDY-AND-WATER.

Of this mixture Charles Lamb said that it spoiled two good things.

LOVE OF THE WONDERFUL.

What stronger pleasure is there with mankind, or what do they earlier learn or longer retain, than *the love of hearing and relating things strange and incredible.* How wonderful a thing is *the love of wondering* and *of raising wonder!* 'Tis the delight of children to hear tales they shiver at, and the vice of old men to abound in strange stories of times past. We come into the world wondering at every thing; and when our wonder about common things is over, we seek something new to wonder at. Our last scene is to tell wonders of *our own*, to all who will believe them. And amidst all this, 'tis well if truth comes off but moderately tainted.—*Shaftesbury.*

CLERICAL FOPS.

There is a class of fops not usually designated by that epithet—men clothed in profound black, with large canes, and strange, amorphous hats—of big speech, and imperative presence—talkers about Plato—great affecters of senility—despisers of women, and all the graces of life—fierce foes to common-sense—abusive of the living, and approving no one who has not been dead for at least a century. Such fops, as vain and as shallow as their fraternity in Bond-street, differ from these only as Gorgonius differed from Rufillus.—*Sydney Smith.*

LYING.

Although the devil be the father of lies, he seems, like other great inventors, to have lost much of his reputation, by the continual improvements that have been made upon him.—*Swift.*

THE HEALTHY MAN.

Of all the know-nothing persons in this world, commend us to the man who has "never known a day's illness." He is a moral dunce, one who has lost the greatest lesson in life; who has skipped the finest lecture in that great school of humanity, the sick-chamber. Let him be versed in mathematics, profound in metaphysics, a ripe scholar in the classics, a bachelor of arts, or even a doctor in divinity; yet is he as one of those gentlemen whose education has been neglected. For all his college acquirements, how inferior is he in useful knowledge to a mortal who has had but a quarter's gout, or half a year's ague—how infinitely below the fellow-creature who has been soundly taught his tic-douloureux, thoroughly grounded in the rheumatics, and deeply *red* in scarlet fever! And yet, what is more common than to hear a great hulking, florid fellow, bragging of an ignorance, a brutal ignorance, that he shares in common with the pig and bullock, the generality of which die, probably, without ever having experienced a day's indisposition?—*Hood.*

PLAIN TRUTH.

One of the sublimest things in the world, is plain truth!—*Bulwer.*

SELF-IMPORTANCE.

Of such mighty importance every man is to himself, and ready to think he is so to others; without once making this easy and obvious reflection, that his affairs can have no more weight with other men than theirs have with him; and how little that is, he is sensible enough.—*Swift.*

MISERS.

The passion for wealth has worn out much of its grossness by tract of time. Our ancestors certainly conceived of money as able to confer a distinct gratification in itself, not alone considered simply as a symbol of wealth. The oldest poets, when they introduce a miser, constantly make him address his gold as his mistress; as something to be seen, felt, and hugged; as capable of satisfying two of the senses at least. The substitution of a thin, unsatisfying medium for the good old tangible gold, has made avarice quite a Platonic affection in comparison with the seeing, touching, and handling pleasures of the old Chrysophilities. A bank-note can no more satisfy the touch of a true sensualist in this passion, than Creusa could return her husband's embrace in the shades.

A miser is sometimes a grand personification of Fear. He has a fine horror of Poverty; and he is not content to keep Want from the door, or at arm's length—but he places it, by heaping wealth upon wealth, *at a sublime distance!*—*Lamb.*

TAVERNS.

Dr. Johnson breaks out into a high encomium upon taverns: "There is no private house," he remarks, "in which people can enjoy themselves so well as at a capital tavern. Let there be ever so great plenty of good things, ever so much grandeur, ever so much elegance, ever so much desire that every body should be easy, in the nature of things it cannot be: there must always be some degree of care and anxiety. The master of the house is anxious to entertain his guests; the guests are anxious to be agreeable to him; and no man, but a very impudent dog indeed, can as freely command what is in another man's house as if it were his own: whereas, in a tavern, there is a general freedom from anxiety. You are sure you are welcome; and the more noise you make, the more trouble you give, the more good things you call for, the welcomer you are. No servant will attend you with the alacrity which waiters do, who are incited by the prospect of an immediate reward in proportion as they please. No, sir; there is nothing which has yet been contrived by man, by which so much happiness is produced, as by a good tavern or inn."

Archbishop Leighton used often to say, that if he were to choose a place to die in, it should be an inn.

MISTAKE ON BOTH SIDES.

Voltaire was one day speaking warmly in praise of the physician Haller, in presence of a person who was living in his house. "Ah, sir," said this person, "if M. Haller would but speak of your works as you speak of his." "Possibly we are both mistaken," said Voltaire.

PRESENTS.

If presents be not the soul of friendship, doubtless they are the most spiritual part of the body in that intercourse. There is too much narrowness of thinking on this point! The punctilio of acceptance, methinks, is too confined and straitened. I should be content to receive money, or clothes, or a joint of meat from a friend. Why should he not send me a dinner as well as a dessert? I would taste him in the beasts of the field, and through all creation.—*Lamb.*

INFANTS.

Some admiring what motives to mirth infants meet with in their silent and solitary smiles, have resolved, how truly I know not, that they converse with angels; as, indeed, such cannot among mortals find any fitter companions.—*Fuller.*

DISCRETION.

There is no talent so useful towards rising in the world, or which puts men more out of the reach of fortune, than that quality generally possessed by the dullest sort of men, and in common speech called discretion; a species of lower prudence, by the assistance of which, people of the meanest intellects, without any other qualification, pass through the world in great tranquillity, and with universal good treatment, neither giving nor taking offence.—*Swift.*

INTELLIGIBILITY.

It would be well, both for the public and the writers themselves, if some authors would but adopt Lord Falkland's method, before publishing his works, who, when he doubted whether a word was perfectly intelligible or not, used to consult one of his lady's chambermaids, (not the waiting-woman, because it was possible she might be conversant in romances,) and by her judgment was guided whether to receive or reject it. Swift pursued, it is said, a like method of reading his works to the *unlearned.*

ANTIQUITY OF AGRICULTURE.

The first three men in the world were a gardener, a ploughman, and a grazier; and if any man object that the second of these was a murderer, I desire he would consider, that as soon as he was so, he quitted our profession and turned builder.—*Cowley.*

MR. PERKINS, THE DIVINE.

He had a capacious head, with angles winding and roomy enough for all controversial intricacies. He would pronounce the word *damn*, with such an emphasis as left a doleful echo in his auditor's ears a good while afterward.—*Fuller.*

SUSPICION.

Always to think the worst, I have ever found to be the mark of a mean spirit and a base soul.—*Bolingbroke.*

CANNIBALS.

Lamb writes to his friend Manning, to dissuade him from going to China, and endeavours to instill the fear of cannibals into his mind. "Some say the Tartars are cannibals, and then conceive a fellow *eating* my friend, and adding the *cool malignity* of mustard and vinegar." This reminds one of the advice Sydney Smith is said to have given to the bishop of New Zealand, previous to his departure recommending him to have regard to the minor as well as to the more grave duties of his station—to be given to hospitality—and, in order to meet the tastes of his native guests, never to be without a smoked little boy in the bacon-rack, and a cold clergyman on the sideboard. "And as for myself, my lord," he concluded, "all I can say is, that when your new parishioners *do* eat you, I hope you will disagree with them."

FLOGGING AT SCHOOL.

If the dead have any cognizance of posthumous fame, one would think it must abate somewhat of the pleasures with which Virgil and Ovid regard their earthly immortality, when they see to what base purposes their productions are employed. That their voices should be administered to boys in regular doses, as lessons or impositions, and some dim conception whipped into the tail when it has failed to penetrate the head, cannot be just the sort of homage to their genius which they anticipated or desired.—*The Doctor.*

A DINNER-PARTY.

An excellent and well-arranged dinner, is a most pleasing occurrence, and a great triumph of civilized life. It is not only the descending morsel and the enveloping sauce, but the rank, wealth, wit, and beauty which surround the meats; the learned management of light and heat; the silent and rapid services of the attendants; the smiling and sedulous host, proffering gusts and relishes; the exotic bottles; the embossed plate; the pleasant remarks; the handsome dresses; the cunning artifices in fruit and farina! The hour of dinner, in short, includes every thing of sensual and intellectual gratification, which a great nation glories in producing.—*Sydney Smith.*

LITERARY ENTERTAINMENTS.

Menage makes mention of a person, who occasionally gave entertainments to authors. His fancy was to place them at table, each according to the size and thickness of the volumes they had published, commencing with the folio authors, and proceeding through the quarto and octavo, down to the duodecimo, each according to his rank.

DULLNESS.

"A man," said Tom Brown, "is never ruined by dullness."

SCOLDING AND QUARRELLING

Have something of *familiarity* and a commnnity of interest; they imply acquaintance; they are of one sentiment, which is of the family of dearness. —*Lamb.*

HUMAN LIFE.

When all is done, human life is, at the greatest and the best, but like a froward child that must be played with and humoured a little to keep it quiet till it falls asleep, and then the care is over.—*Sir William Temple.*

THE ENGLISH LANGUAGE.

They may talk as they will of the dead languages. Our auxiliary verbs give us a power which the ancients, with all their varieties of mood, and inflections of tense, never could obtain.—*The Doctor.*

EXCUSE FOR A LONG LETTER.

In a postscript to one of the "Provincial Letters," Pascal excuses himself for the letter being so long, on the plea that he had not had time to make it shorter.

REAL MANNERS.

Good manners is the art of making those people easy with whom we converse. Whoever makes the fewest persons uneasy, is the best bred in the company.—*Swift.*

ECCENTRIC TASTE.

George Selwyn was noted for a passion for the details of criminal justice, from "the warrant to the rope;" and his friends always made it a point of gratifying this peculiarity, by sending him news of criminals, executions, &c. When Horace Walpole's house in Arlington-street was broken open, he dispatched a messenger to Selwyn, to inform him of the fact, and of his having secured the thief. It happened that the person who received the message had lately been robbed himself, and had the wound fresh in his mind. "He stalked up into the club-room," relates Walpole, "stopped short, and with a hollow trembling voice said, 'Mr. Selwyn, Mr. Walpole's compliments, and he's got a housebreaker for you.'"

JOHN RANDOLPH.

The celebrated John Randolph not wishing to reply to a disagreeable question put to him in Congress, evaded it by saying, "Sir, that is a question, and I never answer questions."

DUELLING,

Though barbarous in civilized, is a highly civilized institution among barbarous people; and when compared to assassination, is a prodigious victory gained over human passions.—*Sydney Smith.*

NARROW-MINDED PERSON.

Dr. Franklin, talking of a friend of his who had been a Manchester dealer, said, "that he never sold a piece of tape narrower than his own mind."

FASTIDIOUS TASTES.

A fastidious taste is like a squeamish appetite: the one has its origin in some disease of the mind, as the other has in some ailment of the stomach.—*The Doctor.*

ILL-NATURED PERSONS.

If thou be a severe, sour-complexioned man, then here I disallow thee to be a competent judge.—*Isaak Walton.*

EMPTY MINDS.

Some men do wisely to counterfeit a reservedness, to keep their chests always locked, not for fear any one should steal treasure thence, but lest some one should look in and see, that there is nothing within them.—*Fuller.*

BURNING CHIMNEY-SWEEPS.

A large party are invited to dinner, a great display is to be made; and about an hour before dinner, there is an alarm that the kitchen chimney is on fire! It is impossible to put off the distinguished persons who are expected. It gets very late for the soup and fish; the cook is frantic; all eyes are turned upon the sable consolation of the master chimney-sweeper; and up into the midst of the burning chimney is sent one of the miserable little infants of the brush! There is a positive prohibition of this practice, and an enactment of penalties in one of the acts of parliament which respect chimney-sweepers. But what matters acts of parliament, when the pleasures of genteel people are concerned? Or what is a toasted child, compared to the agonies of the mistress of the house with a deranged dinner.—*Sydney Smith.*

BUTLER'S WIT.

The earl of Dorset, having a great desire to pass an evening with Butler, as a private gentleman, prevailed upon a common friend, Mr. Shepherd, to introduce him into his company at a tavern to which they both resorted. This being done, Butler, while the first bottle was being drunk, appeared very flat and heavy; at the second bottle extremely brisk and lively, abounding in wit and learning, and making himself a most agreeable companion; when the third bottle was finished, he again sank into such stupidity and dullness, that hardly any body could have believed him to be the author of Hudibras. The next day, the earl of Dorset was asked his opinion of him; he answered, "He is like a ninepin, little at both ends, but great in the middle."

THE PROTESTANT CHURCH.

John Wilkes was once asked by a Roman Catholic gentleman, in a warm dispute on religion, "Where was your church before Luther?" "Did you wash your face this morning?" inquired the facetious alderman. "I did, sir." "Then pray, where was your face before it was washed?"

THE POWER OF HABIT.

The power of habit is exemplified in the case of Jonathan Wild and Count Fathom; Mr. Wild could not keep his hands out the Count's pockets, although he knew they were empty; nor could the Count abstain from palming a card, although he was well aware Wild had no money to pay him.

ESSAYS ON TASTE.

There are some readers who have never read an essay on taste, and if they take my advice they never will; for they can no more improve their taste by so doing, than they could improve their appetite or digestion by studying a cookery book.—*The Doctor.*

EMPTY AND CROWDED CHURCH.

In the latter, it is chance but some present human frailty—an act of inattention on the part of some of the auditory—or a trait of affectation, or, worse, vain glory on that of the preacher—puts us by our best thoughts, disharmonizing the place and the occasion. But wouldst thou know the beauty of holiness? go alone on some week day, borrowing the keys of good master sexton; traverse the cool aisles of some country church; think of the piety that has knelt there—the congregations, old and young, that have found consolation there—the meek pastor—the docile parishioners — with no disturbing emotions, no cross conflicting comparisons, drink in the tranquillity of the place, till thou thyself, become fixed as the marble effigies that kneel and weep around thee.—*Lamb.*

TEDIOUS PERSONS.

A tedious person is one a man would leap a steeple from.—*Ben Jonson.*

MORTALITY.

To smell to a turf of fresh earth, is wholesome for the body; no less are thoughts of mortality cordial to the soul. "*Earth thou art, to earth thou shalt return.*"—*Fuller.*

LATE HOURS.

Mr. Barham, author of the Ingolsby Legends, when a youth, studied with Mr. Hodson, afterward principal of Brazennose. This gentleman, who, doubtless discerning, spite of an apparent levity, much that was amiable and high-minded in his pupil, treated him with marked indulgence, sent, however, on one occasion, to demand an explanation of his continued absence from morning chapel. "The fact is, sir," urged his pupil, "you are too late for me." "Too late!" repeated the tutor, in astonishment. "Yes, sir; I cannot sit up till seven o'clock in the morning; I am a man of regular habits, and unless I get to bed by four or five at latest, I am really fit for nothing next day."

THE BEST STYLE.

Take this, reader, for a general rule, that the readiest and plainest style is the most forcible, (if the head be but properly stored,) and that in all ordinary cases, the word which first presents itself is the best.—*The Doctor.*

When a man's thoughts are clear, the properest words will generally offer themselves first, and his own judgment will direct him in what order to place them, so as they may be best understood.

NOTES OF ADMIRATION.

Swift mentions a gentleman, who made it a rule in reading, to skip over all sentences where he spied a note of admiration at the end.

THE BEST KIND OF ACID.

Martin Burney was one day explaining the three kinds of acid, very *lengthily*, to Charles Lamb, when the latter stopped him by saying: "The best of all kind of acid, however, as you know, Martin, is uity —assiduity."

BREVITY.

These are my thoughts; I might have spun them out to a greater length, but I think a little *plot* of ground, thick sown, is better than a great field, which, for the most part of it, lies fallow.—*Norris.*

CHILDREN.

"Oh! what blockheads are those wise persons," exclaims Southey, "who think it necessary that a child should comprehend every thing it reads."

OLD ANGELS.

A traveller arriving at the town of Doncaster one evening late in the autumn, alighted at the Old Angel Inn. "The *Old* Angel!" said he to his fellow-traveller; "you see that even angels on earth grow old."

NATURE.

All things are artificial, for nature is the art of God.—*Sir Thomas Browne.*

IDLENESS.

Too much idleness, I have observed, fills up a man's time much more completely, and leaves him less his own master, than any sort of employment whatsoever.—*Burke.*

WIT AND THE GREATER PASSIONS.

It must be observed that all the great passions, and many other feelings, extinguish the relish for wit. Thus *lympha pudica Deum vidit et erebuit* would be witty, were it not bordering on the sublime. The resemblance between the sandal-tree imparting (while it falls) its aromatic flavour to the edge of the axe, and the benevolent man rewarding evil with good, would be witty, did it not excite virtuous emotions. There are many mechanical contrivances which excite sensations very similar to wit, but the attention is absorbed by their utility. Some of Merlin's machines, which have no utility at all, are quite similar to wit. A small model of a steam-engine, or mere squirt, is wit to a child. A man speculates upon the causes of the first, or on its consequences, and so loses the feelings of wit: with the latter he is too familiar to be surprised. In short, the essence of every species of wit is surprise; which *vi termini,* must be sudden; and the sensations which wit has a tendency to excite, are impaired or destroyed, as often as they are mingled with much thought or passion.—*Sydney Smith.*

SCHOOL LEARNING.

I am sometimes inclined to think that pigs are brought up upon a wiser system than boys at a grammar-school. The pig is allowed to feed upon any kind of offal, however coarse, on which he can thrive, till the time approaches, when pig is to commence pork, or take a degree as bacon.—*The Doctor.*

DIFFERENCE OF OPINION.

I could never divide myself from any man upon the difference of an opinion, or be angry with his judgment for not agreeing in that from which within a few days I might dissent myself.—*Sir Thomas Browne.*

GREAT MEN.

The true test of a great man—that at least which must secure his place among the highest order of great men—is his having been in advance of his age. This it is which decides whether or not he has carried forward the grand plan of human improvement; has conformed his views and adapted his conduct to the existing circumstances of society, or changed those so as to better its condition; has been one of the lights of the world, or only reflected the borrowed rays of former luminaries; and sat in the same shade with the rest of his generation, at the same twilight or the same dawn.—*Brougham.*

THE PYRAMIDS,

Doting with age, have forgotten the names of their founders.—*Fuller.*

CONVERSATION OF PHILOSOPHERS.

A philosopher's ordinary language and admissions in general conversations or writings, *ad populum*, are as his watch compared with his astronomical time-piece. He sets the former by the town clock, not because he believes it right, but because his neighbours and his cook go by it.—*Coleridge.*

PREACHING DAMNATION.

"To preach long, loud, and damnation, is the way," says Selden, "to be cried up: we love a man that damns us, and we run after him again to save us!"

MODERATION.

Fuller beautifully says of moderation, that "it is the silken string running through the pearl chain of all virtues."

WILKIE AND THE MONK OF THE ESCURIAL.

When Wilkie was in the Escurial, looking at Titian's famous picture of the Last Supper in the refectory there, an old Jeronimite said to him, "I have sat daily in sight of that picture for now nearly threescore years: during that time my companions have dropped off, one after another, all who were my seniors, all who were my contemporaries, and many or most of those who were younger than myself; more than one generation has passed away, and there the figures in the picture have remained, unchanged! I look at them till I sometimes think that they are the realities, and we but shadows."—*The Doctor.*

MR. FIEVÉE.

We must do justice to Mr. Fievée when he deserves it. He evinces, in his preface, a lurking uneasiness at the apprehension of exciting war between the two countries, from the anger to which his letters will give birth in England. He pretends to deny that they will occasion a war; but it is very easy to see he is not convinced by his own arguments; and we confess ourselves extremely pleased by this amiable solicitude at the probable effusion of human blood. We hope Mr. Fievée is deceived by his philanthropy, and that no such unhappy consequences will ensue, as he really believes, though he affects to deny them. We dare say the dignity of England will be satisfied, if the publication in question is disowned by the French government, or, at most, if the author is given up. At all events, we have no scruple to say, that to sacrifice twenty thousand lives, and a hundred millions of money, to resent Mr. Fievée's book, would be an unjustifiable waste of blood and treasure; and that to take him off privately by assassination would be an undertaking hardly compatible with the dignity of a great empire.

Mr. Fievée alleges against the English, that they have great pleasure in contemplating the spectacle of men deprived of their reason; and indeed we must have the candour to allow, that the hospitality which Mr. Fievée experienced seems to afford pretext for this assertion.—*Sydney Smith.*

PRIVATE FAMILY HISTORY.

The history of any private family, however humble, could it be fully related for five or six generations, would illustrate the state and progress of society better than could be done by the most elaborate dissertation.—*The Doctor.*

A POPULAR FALLACY.

When the world has once got hold of a lie, it is astonishing how hard it is to get it out of the world. You beat it about the head, till it seems to have given up the ghost, and lo! the next day it is as healthy as ever.—*Bulwer.*

ENGLISHMEN.

An Englishman is essentially, not only a cooking and a tailoring animal, according to the definition of man given by some philosophers, but in his special Anglican capacity, he is pre-eminently a grumbling animal. We go further: we believe that this grumbling habit, and the feeling from which it proceeds, are among the active causes of his progressive improvement. Discontented with his condition he seeks to improve it. Finding fault with the constitution of his country, he vigorously but wisely reforms it. He quarrels with his house, and he builds it in a better site and on a more commodious scale. The excellent Count Strzelecki observed, in his evidence before the Lords, "the Irish soon improve in the colonies; they become quite as grumbling as the English themselves." This observation displays a true knowledge of the national character. We love to believe that we are on the verge of ruin; and we readily attribute our supposed ruin to the legislature, or to the government of the day.—*Edinburgh Review.*

A GOOD STOMACH.

What an excellent thing did God bestow on man, when He did give him a good stomach.—*Beaumont and Fletcher.*

LOVERS OF LITERATURE.

Your true lover of literature is never fastidious. I do not mean the *helluo librorum*, the swinish feeder, who thinks that every name which is to be found in a title-page, or on a tombstone, ought to be rescued from oblivion; nor those first cousins of the moth, who labour under a bulimy for black-letter, and believe every thing to be excellent which was written in the reign of Elizabeth. I mean the man of robust and healthy intellect, who gathers the harvest of literature into his barns, thrashes the straw, winnows the grain, grinds it at his own mill, bakes it in his own oven, and then eats the true bread of knowledge. If he bake his loaf upon a cabbage-leaf, and eat onions with his bread and cheese, let who will find fault with him for his taste—not I!—*The Doctor.*

VIRTUE IN A SHORT PERSON.

His soul had but a short diocese to visit, and therefore might the better attend the effectual informing thereof.—*Fuller.*

ENJOYMENT OF LIFE.

Ennui, wretchedness, melancholy, groans, and sighs, are the offering which these unhappy Methodists make to a Deity, who has covered the earth with gay colours, and scented it with rich perfumes; and shown us, by the plan and order of his works, that he has given to man something better than a bare existence, and scattered over his creation a thousand superfluous joys, which are totally unnecessary to the mere support of life.—*Sydney Smith.*

CLASSIFICATION OF NOVELS.

Novels may be arranged according to the botanical system of Linnæus. Monandria Monogynia is the usual class, most novels having one hero and one heroine. Sir Charles Grandison belongs to the Monandria Digynia. Those in which the families of the two lovers are at variance, may be called Diœcious. The Cryptogamia are very numerous, so are the Polygamia. Where the lady is in doubt which of her lovers to choose, the tale is to be classed under the Icosandria. Where the party hesitates between love and duty, or avarice and ambition, Didynamia. Many are poisonous, few of any use, and far the greater number of annuals.—*Southey's Omnia.*

PAMPHLETS AND BALLADS.

Though some may make light of libels,* yet you may see by them how the wind sets; as take a straw, and throw it up into the air, you shall see by that which way the wind is, which you shall not do by casting up a stone; more solid things do not show the complexion of the times so well as ballads and libels.—*Selden's Table-Talk.*

ANCESTRY.

"The man who has not any thing to boast of but his illustrious ancestors," says Sir Thomas Overbury, "is like a potato—the only good belonging to him is under ground."

The duke of Somerset, surnamed the Proud Duke, and of whom it is related that he rode all

* Pamphlets.

through Europe, without ever leaning back in his carriage, used to say, "that he pitied Adam, because he had no ancestors."

ELEGANCE

Is something more than ease; it is more than a freedom from awkwardnesss or restraint. It implies, I conceive, a precision, a polish, a sparkling, spirited yet delicate.—*Hazlitt.*

RICHARD L. EDGEWORTH.

The "Essay upon Bulls" is written much with the same mind, and in the same manner, as a schoolboy takes a walk: he moves on the straight road for ten yards, with surprising perseverance; then sets out after a butterfly, looks for a bird's nest, and jumps backward and forward over a ditch. In the same manner, this nimble and digressive gentleman is away after every object which crosses his mind. If you leave him at the end of a comma, in a steady pursuit of his subject, you are sure to find him, before the next full stop, a hundred yards to the right or left, frisking, capering, and grinning, in a high paroxysm of merriment and agility. Mr. Edgeworth seems to possess the sentiments of an accomplished gentleman, the information of a scholar, and the vivacity of a first-rate harlequin. He is fuddled with animal spirits, giddy with constitutional joy: in such a state, he must have written on or burst.—*Sydney Smith.*

VANITY OF HUMAN FAME.

An old woman in a village of the west of England was told one day that the king of Prussia was dead, such a report having arrived when the great Frederick was in the noonday of his glory. Old Mary lifted up her great slow eyes at the news, and fixing them in the fullness of vacancy upon her informant, replied, "Is a! is a! the Lord ha' mercy! Well, well! the king of Prussia! and who's he?" The "who's he?" of this old woman might serve as text for a notable sermon upon ambition. "Who's he?" may now be asked of men greater as soldiers in their day than Frederick and Wellington; greater as discoverers than Sir Isaac or Sir Humphrey. Who built the pyramids? Who ate the first oyster? *Vanitas vanitatum! Omnia vanitas!*—*The Doctor.*

FRENCH AND ENGLISH VANITY.

The vanity of a Frenchman consists (as I have somewhere read) in belonging to so great a country; but the vanity of an Englishman exults in the thought that so great a country belongs to himself. The root of all English notions, as of all English laws, is to be found in the sentiment of property. It is *my* wife whom you shall not insult; it is *my* house that you shall not enter; it is *my* country that you shall not traduce; and by a species of ultra-mundane appropriation, it is *my* God whom you shall not blaspheme! —*England and the English.*

POCKETS.

Of all the inventions of the tailor, (who is of all artists the most inventive,) I hold the pocket to be the most commodious, and, saving the fig-leaf, the most indispensable. Moreover, nature herself shows us the utility, the importance, nay, the indispensability, or, to take a hint from the pure language of our diplomatists, the *sinequanonniness* of pockets. There is but one organ which is common to all animals whatsoever: some are without eyes, many without noses; some have no heads, others no tails; some neither one nor the other; some there are who have no brains, others very pappy ones; some no hearts, others very bad ones: but all have a stomach; and what is the stomach but a live inside pocket? Hath not Van Helmont said of it, "*Saccus vel vera est, ut ciborum olla?*"—*The Doctor.*

CHOICE OF BOOKS.

They unto whom we shall appear tedious, are in no wise injured by us, because it is in their own hands to spare that labour which they are not willing to endure.—*Hooker.*

SCHOOLMASTERS.

A schoolmaster, who likes his vocation, feels towards the boys who deserve his favour something like a thrifty and thriving father towards the children for whom he is scraping together wealth; he is contented that his humble and patient industry should produce fruit, not for himself, but for them, and looks with pride to a result in which it is impossible for him to partake, and which in all likelihood he may never live to see.—*The Doctor.*

WIT AND JUDGMENT.

Wit is brushwood, judgment timber: the one gives the greatest flame, the other yields the durablest heat; and both meeting make the best fire.—*Sir Thomas Overbury.*

CURATES.

A curate—there is something which excites compassion in the very name of a curate!!! How any man of purple, palaces, and preferment, can let himself loose upon this poor workingman of God, we are at a loss to conceive,—a learned man in a hovel, with sermons and saucepans, lexicons and bacon, Hebrew books and ragged children; good and patient; a comforter and a preacher; the first and purest pauper in the hamlet, and yet showing, that, in the midst of his worldly misery, he has the heart of a gentleman, the spirit of a Christian, and the kindness of a pastor.—*Sydney Smith.*

FATE OF POETS.

"I have met with most poetry upon trunks," says Lord Byron; "so that I am apt to consider the trunk-maker as the sexton of authorship."

OPINION.

An originator of an opinion precedes the time; you cannot both precede and reflect it. What ten years ago was philosophy, is now opinion.—*Bulwer.*

CONVERSATION.

The art of quiet, entertaining, easy conversation, is, I think, chiefly known in England. In Scotland we are pedantic and wrangle, or we run away with the harrows on some topic we chance to be discursive upon. In Ireland, they have too much vivacity, and are too desirous to make a show to preserve the golden mean. They are the Gascons of Britain. For forming a good converser, good taste, and extensive information and accomplishment, are the principal requisites; to which must be added an easy and elegant delivery, and a well-toned voice.—*Sir Walter Scott.*

WISDOM OF MIRTH.

I have observed, that in comedy, the best actor plays the part of the droll, while some scrub rogue is made the hero, or fine gentleman. So, in this farce of life, wise men pass their time in mirth, whilst fools only are serious.—*Bolingbroke.*

STRAWBERRY HILL.

One of Walpole's most favourite pursuits, was the building and decoration of his gothic villa of Strawberry Hill. It is situated at the end of the village of

Twickenham, towards Teddington, on a slope, which gives it a fine view of a reach of the Thames, and the opposite wooded hill of Richmond Park. He bought it, in 1747, of Mrs. Chenevix, the proprietress of a celebrated toy-shop. He thus describes it, in a letter of that year to Mr. Conway: "You perceive, by my date, that I have got into a new camp, and have left my tub at Windsor. It is a little plaything house that I got out of Mrs. Chenevix's shop, and is the prettiest bauble you ever saw. It is set in enamelled meadows with fillagree hedges:

'A small Euphrates through the piece is roll'd,
And little fishes wave their wings of gold.'

"Two delightful roads, that you would call dusty, supply me continually with coaches and chaises; barges, as solemn as barons of the Exchequer, move under my window; Richmond Hill and Ham Walks bound my prospects, but, thank God! the Thames is between me and the duchess of Queensbury. Dowagers, as plenty as flounders, inhabit all around; and Pope's ghost is just now skimming under my window by most poetical moonlight."

After his villa had been built, he commenced to collect antiquities and curiosities of all kinds, together with many valuable paintings and engravings, which he seems to have spared no expense in buying and bringing together. Here, also, he had set up a small printing-press, with which he printed many of his own works, and those of his friends. Gray's poems were printed here, with engravings by Mr. Richard Bently, a friend of both authors. For defraying these expenses, he drew upon his income, which amounted to about two thousand pounds a year, chiefly arising from the various sinecures conferred upon him by his father, Sir Robert Walpole.

This fine collection, upon which he had employed so much pains, and expended such large sums of money, is now scattered to the winds—dispersed at a public sale. Surely, it is enough

"To rouse the dead man into rage,
And warm with red resentment the wan cheek."

BULLS.

A bull is exactly the counterpart of a witticism: for as wit discovers real relations that are not apparent, bulls admit apparent relations that are not real. The pleasure arising from bulls, proceeds from our surprise at suddenly discovering two things to be dissimilar in which a resemblance might have been suspected. The same doctrine will apply to wit and bulls in action. Practical wit discovers connection or relation between actions, in which duller understandings discover none; and practical bulls originate from an apparent relation between two actions which more correct understandings immediately perceive to have none at all. In the late rebellion in Ireland, the rebels, who had conceived a high degree of indignation against some great banker, passed a resolution that they would burn his notes;—which they accordingly did, with great assiduity; forgetting, that in burning his notes, they were destroying his debts, and that for every note which went into the flames, a correspondent value went into the banker's pocket. A gentleman in speaking of a nobleman's wife, of great rank and fortune, lamented very much that she had no children. A medical gentleman who was present observed, that to have no children was a great misfortune, but he thought he had remarked it was *hereditary* in some families. Take any instance of this branch of the ridiculous, and you will always find an apparent relation of ideas leading to a complete inconsistency. There are some bulls so extremely fallacious, that any man may imagine himself to have been betrayed into them; but these are rare: and, in general, it is a poor contemptible species of amusement; a delight in which evinces a very bad taste in wit.—*Sydney Smith.*

PREACHING AND PRACTICE.

Dr. Channing had a brother, a physician, and at one time they both lived in Boston. One day, a countryman in search of a *divine*, knocked at the *doctor's* door, when the following dialogue ensued:—

"Does Mr. Channing live here?"

"Yes, sir."

"Can I see him?"

"I am he."

"Who—you?"

"Yes, sir."

"You must have altered considerably since I heard you preach!"

"Oh, I see your mistake now. It's my brother who *preaches*. I *practise*."

LOVE OF MONEY.

"Mirabeau," said Rivarol, "is capable of any thing for money; even a good action."

MARK OF GENIUS.

Many persons think it a mark of genius to be eccentric, and to depart from the common road, or to do things in an uncommon way, like the lady in Pope's works, who drank her tea by stratagem; or like Hudibras, who could wisely tell—

————"what hour o' the day
The clock does strike, by algebra."

INDESTRUCTIBILITY OF ENJOYMENT.

Mankind are always happier for having been happy; so that if you make them happy now, you make them happy twenty years hence, by the memory of it. A childhood passed with a due mixture of rational indulgence, under fond and wise parents, diffuses over the whole of life a feeling of calm pleasure; and, in extreme old age, is the very last remembrance which time can erase from the mind of man. No enjoyment, however inconsiderable, is confined to the present moment. A man is the happier for life, from having made once an agreeable tour, or lived for any length of time with pleasant people, or enjoyed any considerable interval of innocent pleasure; which contributes to render old men so inattentive to the scenes before them, and carries them back to a world that is past, and to scenes never to be renewed again.—*Sydney Smith.*

HANDWRITING.

Hood gives some good advice upon this subject, which he submits to the particular attention of "poets and prosers, who aspire to write in miscellanies; and, above all, the palpitating untried, who meditate the offer of their maiden essays to established periodicals." He advises these writers, to "take care to cultivate a good, plain, bold, round text; to set up Tomkins as well as Pope or Dryden for a model, and to have an eye to their pot-hooks.

"Of all things, therefore, be legible; and to that end, practise in penmanship. If you have never learned, take six lessons of Mr. Carstairs. Be sure to buy the best paper, the best ink, the best pens, and then sit down and do the best you can; as the schoolboys do—put out your tongue, and take pains. So ye shall haply escape the rash rejection of a jaded editor; so, having got in your hand, it is possible that your head may follow; and so, last not least, ye may fortunately avert those awful mistakes of the press, which sometimes ruin a poet's sublimest effusion, by pantomimically transforming his 'roses' into 'noses;' his 'angels' into 'angles;' and all his 'happiness' into 'pappiness.'"

PATRIOTISM.

"Patriots," said Sir Robert Walpole, "are easily raised; I have myself, made many a one. 'Tis but to refuse an unreasonable demand, and up springs a patriot."

This is in the spirit of Tom Brown's saying: "A patriot is generally made by a pique at court."

PUNCH.

That Punch made his appearance in the puppet-show of the Deluge, most persons know; his exclamation of "Hazy weather, master Noah!" having been preserved by tradition.—*The Doctor.*

CLASS OF CONVERSATIONALISTS.

Swift describes a class of tiresome conversationalists, who should be driven from all pleasant society: these are "people who think they sufficiently acquit themselves, and entertain their company, with relating facts of no consequence, nor at all out of the road of such common incidents as happen every day." He then proceeds, with some illiberality: "and this I have observed more frequently among the Scots than any other nation, who are very careful not to omit the minutest circumstances of time or place; which kind of discourse, if it were not a little relieved by the uncouth terms and phrases, as well as accent and gesture, peculiar to that country, would be hardly tolerable."

PUNS.

I have mentioned puns. They are, I believe, what I have denominated them—the wit of words. They are exactly the same to words that wit is to ideas, and consist in the sudden discovery of relations in language. A pun, to be perfection in its kind, should contain two distinct meanings; the one, common and obvious; the other, more remote; and in the notice which the mind takes of the relation between these two sets of words, and in the surprise which that relation excites, the pleasure of a pun consists. Miss Hamilton, in her book on Education, mentions the instance of a boy so very neglectful, that he never could be brought to read the word *patriarchs;* but whenever he met with it, he pronounced it *partridges.* A friend of the writer, observed to her, that it could hardly be considered a mere piece of negligence, for it appeared to him, that the boy in calling them partridges, was *making game* of the patriarchs. Now, here are two distinct meanings contained in the same phrase: for to make game of the patriarchs is to laugh at them; or to make game of them, is, by a very extravagant and laughable sort of ignorance of words, to rank them among pheasants, partridges, and other such delicacies, which the law takes under its protection, and calls *game;* and the whole pleasure derived from this pun, consists in the sudden discovery, that two such different meanings are referable to one form of expression. I have very little to say about puns; they are in very bad repute, and so they ought to be. The wit of language is so miserably inferior to the wit of ideas, that it is very deservedly driven out of good company. Sometimes, indeed, a pun makes its appearance, which seems, for a moment, to redeem its species; but we must not be deceived by them; it is a radically bad race of wit. By unremitting persecution, it has been at last got under, and driven into cloisters—from whence it must never again be suffered to emerge into the light of the world.—*Sydney Smith.*

TRUE COURTESY.

Nothing is a courtesy, unless it be meant for us, and that friendly and lovingly. We owe no thanks to rivers, that they carry our boats; or winds, that they be favouring, and fill our sails; or meats, that they be nourishing; for these are what they are, necessarily. Horses carry us; trees shade us; but they know it not.—*Ben Jonson.*

ROMAN BANQUETS.

The Roman banquets were much more remarkable for profusion and costliness than for taste. The only merits of a dish composed of the brains of 500 peacocks, or the tongues of 500 nightingales, must have been its dearness; and if a mode of swallowing most money in a given time be the desideratum, commend us to Cleopatra's decoction of diamonds, though even this was fairly exceeded in originality and neatness of conception by the English sailor, who placed a ten-pound note between two slices of bread and butter, and made his black-eyed Susan eat it as a sandwich. Captain Morris, in one of his songs, has set the proper value on such luxuries:—

"Old Lucullus, they say,
Forty cooks had each day,
And Vitellius's meals cost a million;
But I like what is good,
When or where be my food,
In a chop-house or royal pavilion.

"At all feasts, if enough,
I most heartily stuff,
And a song at my heart alike rushes,
Though I've not fed my lungs,
Upon nightingales' tongues,
Nor the brains of gold-finches and thrushes."

Quarterly Review.

LIVING IN THE WORLD.

Living always in the world makes one as unfit for living out of it, as always living out of it does for living in it.—*Walpole.*

SPINNING VIRTUE.

A young preacher, who chose to enlarge to a country congregation on the beauty of virtue, was surprised to be informed by an old woman, who expressed herself highly pleased with his sermon, that her daughter was the most virtuous woman in the parish, "for that week she had spun sax spyndles of yarn."—*Sir Walter Scott.*

UNTHINKING GOOD MAN'S SOUL.

O what a beautiful *concordia discordantium* is an unthinking good man's soul!—*Coleridge.*

CLASSICAL GLORY.

Dr. George, the celebrated Grecian, upon hearing the praises of the great king of Prussia, entertained considerable doubts whether the king, with all his victories, knew how to conjugate a Greek verb in μ. —*Sydney Smith.*

PLEASING THE PUBLIC.

He who would please posterity must please himself, by choosing his own course. There are only two classes of writers who dare do this, the best and the worst; for this is one of the many cases in which extremes meet. The mediocres, in every grade, aim at pleasing the public, and conform themselves to the fashion of their age, whatever it may be.—*The Doctor.*

GIVING DINNERS.

Bulwer advises persons never to give dinners. "Do not go on that foolish plan which has been laid down by persons who pretend to know life, as a means of popularity—of giving dinners better than other people. Unless you are a very rich man, or a very great man, no folly is equal to that of thinking that you soften the hearts of your friends by soups *à la bisque*, and Vermuth wine at a guinea a bottle! They will go away, saying: 'What right has that fellow to give a better dinner than we do? What a horrid taste! what ridiculous presumption!'"

MATHEWS' DECEPTIVE POWERS.

A true tale is told of the late Charles Mathews, that, personating an eccentric old gentleman, a family friend, he drank tea with his mother without her finding out the cheat.

CHARADES.

Sydney Smith says of them, that if they are made at all, they should be made without benefit of clergy, the offender should be instantly hurried off to execution, and be cut off in the middle of his dullness, without being allowed to explain to the executioner, why his first is like his second, or what is the resemblance between his fourth and his ninth.

APPLICABLE TO IDLERS.

A most curious instance of a change of instinct is mentioned by Darwin. The Bees carried over to Barbadoes and the Western Isles, ceased to lay up any honey after the first year; as they found it not useful to them. They found the weather so fine, and materials for making honey so plentiful, that they quitted their grave, prudent, and mercantile character, became exceedingly profligate and debauched, eat up their capital, resolved to work no more, and amused themselves by *flying about the sugar-houses, and stinging the blacks.*

POPE AND SWIFT.

Swift once said in a letter to one of his friends, that he hated human nature, but all his love was towards individuals: "for instance, I hate the tribe of lawyers, but I love Counsellor such-a-one, and Judge such-a-one. But principally I hate and detest that animal, *man,* although I love Peter, John, Thomas, and so forth.

Pope, on the contrary, said his love was for human nature, and his hatred against particular persons.

Perhaps this little thing illustrates the characters of the two authors.

PLEASURES OF A BOOKWORM.

Southey expatiates, with the relish of a bibliomaniac, upon the delights on opening a box of books:—

"Talk of the happiness of getting a great prize in the lottery! What is that to the opening of a box of books? The joy upon lifting up the cover must be something like what we shall feel when Peter the Porter opens the door up stairs, and says, 'Please to walk in, sir.' That I shall never be paid for my labour according to the current value of time and labour, is tolerably certain; but if any one should offer me £10,000 to forego that labour, I should bid him and his money go to the devil, for twice the sum could not purchase me half the enjoyment."

FUGITIVE VERSES.

It is on such scraps that witlings feed; and it is hard that the world should judge of our housekeeping from what we fling to the dogs.—*Pope to Swift.*

DIRTY HANDS.

Charles Lamb once said to a brother whist-player, Martin Burney, whose hands were none of the cleanest, "Martin, if dirt was trumps what a hand you'd have."

MONTAIGNE'S PLAGIARISMS.

Old Montaigne somewhere in his writings informs us of an ingenious plan of his, of transferring whole sentences from ancient authors, without acknowledgment, that the critics might blunder, by giving *nazardes* to Seneca and Plutarch, while they imagined they *tweaked* his nose.

SLEEPING IN CHURCH.

Query, (demands Swift,) whether churches are not dormitories of the living as well as the dead?

ROUSSEAU AND MADAME D'EPINAY.

Their friendship so formed, proceeded to a great degree of intimacy. Madame d'Epinay admired his genius, and provided him with hats and coats; and, at last, was so far deluded by his declamations about the country, as to fit him up a little hermit cottage, where there were a great many birds, and a great many plants and flowers—and where Rousseau was, as might have heen expected, supremely miserable. His friends from Paris did not come to see him. The postman, the butcher, and the baker, hate romantic scenery; duchesses and marchionesses were no longer found to scramble for him. Among the real inhabitants of the country, the reputation of reading and thinking is fatal to character; and Jean Jacques cursed his own successful eloquence which had sent him from the suppers and flattery of Paris to smell to daffodils, watch sparrows, or project idle saliva into the passing stream.—*Sydney Smith.*

COLERIDGE AND THE JEWS.

I have had a good deal to do with Jews in the course of my life, although I never borrowed any money of them. The other day I was what you call *floored* by a Jew. He passed me several times, crying for old clothes in a most nasal and extraordinary tone I ever heard. At last, I was so provoked that I said to him: "Pray, why can't you say 'old clothes' in a plain way, as I do now?" The Jew stopped, and looking very gravely at me said, in a clear and even fine accent, "Sir, I can say 'old clothes' as well as you can; but if you had to say so ten times a minute, for an hour together, you would say '*ogh clo*,' as I do now;" and so he marched off. I was so confounded with the justice of his retort, that I followed and gave him a shilling, the only one I had.

Once I sat in a coach opposite a Jew; a symbol of old clothes-bags; an Isaiah of Holywell-street. He would close the window; I opened it. He closed it again; upon which, in a very solemn tone, I said to him: "Son of Abraham! thou smellest; son of Isaac! thou art offensive; son of Jacob! thou stinkest foully. See the man in the moon! he is holding his nose at that distance; dost thou think that I, sitting here, can endure it any longer?" My Jew was astounded, opened the window forthwith himself, and said, "he was sorry he did not know before, I was so great a gentleman."—*Coleridge's Table-Talk.*

A LOVE OF LITERATURE.

Were I to pray for a taste which should stand me in stead under every variety of circumstances, and be a source of happiness and cheerfulness to me during life, and a shield against its ills, however things might go amiss, and the world frown upon me, it would be a taste for reading. Give a man this taste, and the means of gratifying it, and you can hardly fail of making him a happy man; unless, indeed, you put into his hand a most perverse selection of books.

You place him in contact with the best society in every period of history,—with the wisest, the wittiest, the tenderest, the bravest, and the purest characters who have adorned humanity. You make him a denizen of all nations, a contemporary of all ages. The world has been created for him.—*Sir John Herschel.*

CHARITY OF A MISER.

An illiterate person, who always volunteered to "go round with the hat," but was suspected of sparing his own pocket, overhearing once a hint to that effect, replied: "Other gentlemen puts down what they thinks proper, and so do I. Charity's a private concern, and what I give is *nothing to nobody.*" —*Hood.*

GOOD ACTIONS.

The greatest pleasure I know, is to do a good action by stealth, and to have it found out by accident. —*Charles Lamb.*

RETIRING TO THE COUNTRY.

Very few men who have gratified, and are gratifying their vanity in a great metropolis, are qualified to quit it. Few have the plain sense to perceive that they must soon inevitably be forgotten—or the fortitude to bear it when they are. They represent to themselves imaginary scenes of deploring friends and dispirited companies—but the ocean might as well regret the drops exhaled by the sunbeams. Life goes on; and whether the absent have retired into a cottage or a grave, is much the same thing. In London as in law, *de non apparentibus, et non existentibus eadem est ratio.*—*Sydney Smith.*

SELFISHNESS.

There are persons who have so far outgrown their catechism, as to believe that their only duty is to themselves.—*The Doctor.*

LORD NORTH.

Lord North's wit appears to have been of a kind peculiarly characteristic and eminently natural; playing easily and without the least effort; perfectly suited to his placid nature, by being what Lord Clarendon says of Charles II., "a pleasant, affable, recommending sort of wit;" wholly unpretending; and so exquisitely suited to the occasion that it never failed of effect, yet so readily produced and so entirely unambitious, that although it had occurred to nobody before, every one wondered it had not suggested itself to all. A few only of his sayings have reached us, and these, as might be expected, are rather things which he had chanced to coat over with some sarcasm or epigram that tended to preserve them; they consequently are far from giving an idea of his habitual pleasantry, and the gayety of thought which generally pervaded his speeches. Thus, when a vehement declaimer, calling aloud for his head, turned around and perceived his victim unconsciously indulging in a soft slumber, and becoming still more exasperated, denounced the Minister as capable of sleeping while he ruined his country—the latter only complained how hard it was to be denied a solace which other criminals so often enjoyed, that of having a night's rest before their fate. When surprised in a like indulgence during the performance of a very inferior artist, who, however, showed equal indignation at so ill-timed a recreation, he contented himself with observing, how hard it was that he should be grudged so very natural a release from considerable suffering; but, as if recollecting himself, added, that it was somewhat unjust in the gentleman to complain of him taking the remedy which he had himself been considerate enough to administer. The same good-humour and drollery quitted him not when in opposition. Every one has heard of the speech which, if it had failed to injure the object of its attack, was very effectual in fixing a name upon its honest and much respected author. On Mr. Martin's proposal to have a starling placed near the chair and taught to repeat the cry of "Infamous coalition!" Lord North coolly suggested that, as long as the worthy member was preserved to them, it would be a needless waste of the public money, since the starling might well perform his office by deputy. That in society such a man must have been the most delightful of companions, may well be supposed. In his family, and in all his private intercourse as in his personal character he was known to be in every respect amiable; of scrupulous integrity and unsullied honour.—*Brougham's Statesmen.*

THEODORE HOOK'S HOAXING.

In a life of the author of the "Ingolsby Legends," prefixed to an edition of that work, is given an account of a humorous hoax, played off by Hook, upon an old lady from the country. It is an extract from "Ingolsby's" diary.

"Hook called, and, in the course of conversation, gave me an account of his going to Lord Melville's trial with a friend. They went early, and were engaged in conversation when the peers began to enter. At this moment, a country-looking lady, whom he afterward found to be a resident at Rye, in Sussex, touched his arm, and said, 'I beg your pardon, sir, but pray, who are those gentlemen in red, now coming in?' 'Those, ma'am,' returned Theodore, 'are the barons of England; in these cases the junior peers always come first.' 'Thank you, sir, much obliged to you. Louisa, my dear, (turning to a girl about fourteen,) tell Jane (about ten) those are the barons of England, and the juniors (that's the youngest, you know) always goes first. Tell her to be sure and remember that when we get home.' 'Dear me, ma!' said Louisa, 'can that gentlemen be one of the *youngest?* I am sure he looks very old.'

Human nature, added Hook, could not stand this; any one, though with no more mischief in him than a dove, must have been excited to a hoax. 'And pray, sir,' continued the lady, 'what gentlemen are these?' pointing to the bishops, who came next in order, in the dress which they wear on state occasions, viz.: the rochet and lawn sleeves over their doctor's robes. 'Gentlemen, madam!' said Hook, 'these are not gentlemen; these are ladies, elderly ladies—dowager peeresses in their own right.' The fair inquirer fixed a penetrating glance upon his countenance, saying, as plainly as an eye can say, 'Are you quizzing me or no?' Not a muscle moved; till, at last, tolerably well satisfied with her scrutiny, she turned round and whispered, 'Louisa, dear, the gentleman says that these are elderly ladies and dowager peeresses in their own right; tell Jane not to forget that.' All went on smoothly, till the Speaker of the House of Commons attracted her attention by the rich embroidery of his robes. 'Pray, sir,' said she, 'and who is that fine looking person opposite?' 'That, madam,' was the answer, 'is Cardinal Wolsey.' 'No, sir,' cried the lady, drawing herself up, and casting at her informant a look of angry disdain, 'we know a little better than that; Cardinal Wolsey has been dead many a good year!' 'No such thing, my dear madam, I assure you,' replied Hook, with a gravity which must have been preternatural; 'it has been, I know, so reported in the country, but without the least foundation; in fact, those rascally newspapers will say any thing.' The good old gentlewoman appeared thunder-struck, opened her eyes to their full extent, and gasped like a dying carp; *vox faucibus hæsit*, seizing a daughter with each hand, she hurried, without a word, from the spot."

KING OF CEYLON.

Sydney Smith, in one of his reviews, relates an amusing incident. Speaking of the king of Ceylon, he says: "He has been known to detain a string of four or five Dutch embassies, till various members of the legation died of old age at his court, while they were expecting an answer to their questions, and a return to their presents; and his majesty once exasperated a little French ambassador to such a degree, by the various pretences under which he kept him at his court, that this lively member of the corps diplomatique, one day, in a furious passion, attacked six or seven of his majesty's largest elephants sword in hand, and would, in all probability, have reduced them to mince-meat, if the poor beasts had not been saved from the unequal combat."

ENGLISH AFTER-DINNER SPEECHES.

The New Monthly Magazine gives the following as an average specimen of this species of eloquence:—"This I may say, gentlemen—that is, perhaps, I may be allowed to observe—to remark, rather as remarkably expressive of—to observe, I would say, as remarkably expressive of my feelings on this occa—on the present occasion—is, gentlemen—that I consider this—I'm sure I need not say—and I say it without hesitation—that this is the proudest moment of my life, (pause.) For, as the fabled bird of poetry, the phœnix, of our immortal bard, derives new vitality from the ashes of, if I may be allowed the expression, an expired and extinct existence, so does the calm serenity of age emanate from the transitory turbulence of youth, (pause.) And, gentlemen—gentlemen, I'm quite sure I need not add—need not add, on the present occasion—what I'm sure you will readily believe, that my feelings are naturally, on the present occasion—that those feelings, I say, may be conceived, or even imagined, but they can neither be described, nor—nor—depicted, (pause.) For, like the poisonous upas, whose deadly and devastating,' &c.—Fluent for two minutes and a half."

TWO EVILS.

"There are only two bad things in this world," says Hannah More, "sin and bile."

RESERVED PERSONS.

Persons extremely reserved are like old enamelled watches, which had painted covers, that hindered your seeing what o'clock it was.—*Walpole.*

RETIREMENT.

It is neither so easy a thing, nor so agreeable a one, as men commonly expect, to dispose of leisure when they retire from the business of the world. Their old occupations cling to them, even when they hope that they have emancipated themselves. Go to any seaport town, and you will see that the sea-captain, who has retired upon his well-earned savings, sets up a weather-cock in full view from his windows, and watches the variations of the wind as duly as when he was at sea, though no longer with the same anxiety. A tallow-chandler, having amassed a fortune, disposed of his business, and took a house in the country, not far from London, that he might enjoy himself; and, after a few months' trial of a holiday life, requested permission of his successor to come into town and assist him on melting days. The keeper of a retail spirit-shop, having in like manner retired from trade, used to employ himself by having one puncheon filled with water, and measuring it off by pints into another. A butcher in a small town, for some little time after he had left off business, informed his old customers, that he meant to kill a lamb once a week, just for amusement.—*The Doctor.*

LICENSED JESTER.

If it were possible to restore dead fashions to life, we would revive the office of jester. It is by the squandering glances of the fool, that the wise man's folly is anatomized with least discomfort. From the professed fool he may receive the reproof without feeling the humiliation of it, and the medicine will not work the worse, but the better, for being administered under the disguise of indulgence or recreation. It would be well, indeed, if every man who, whether in thought or in action, has too much his own way, would keep a licensed jester. All coteries, literary, political, or fashionable, which enjoy the dangerous privilege of leading the tastes and opinions of the little circle which is their world, ought certainly to keep one as part of their establishment. The House of Commons, being at once the most powerful body on the earth, and the most intolerant of criticism, stands especially in need of an officer who may speak out at random, without fear of Newgate. Every philosopher who has a system, every theologian who heads a sect, every projector who gathers a company, every interest that can command a party, would do wisely to retain a privileged jester.—*Edinburgh Review.*

NATURAL CURIOSITIES OF CEYLON.

The usual stories are repeated here, of the immense size and voracious appetite of a certain species of serpent. The best history of this kind we ever remember to have read, was of a serpent killed near one of our settlements, in the East Indies; in whose body they found the chaplain of the garrison, all in black, the Rev. Mr. ——, (somebody or other, whose name we have forgotten,) and who, after having been missing for above a week, was discovered in this very inconvenient situation. The dominions of the king of Candia are partly defended by leeches, which abound in the woods, and from which our soldiers suffered in the most dreadful manner. The Cey-lonese, in compensation for their animated plagues, are endowed with two vegetable blessings, the cocoa-nut-tree and the talipot-tree. The latter affords a prodigious leaf, impenetrable to sun or rain, and large enough to shelter ten men. It is a natural umbrella, and is of as eminent service in that country as a greatcoat-tree would be in this.—*Sydney Smith.*

TENDERNESS OF WIT.

Swift says,—"Nothing is so tender as a piece of wit, and which is apt to suffer so much in the carriage. Some things are extremely witty to-day, or fasting, or in this place, or over a bottle; any of which, by the smallest transposal, is utterly annihilated. Thus, wit has its walks and purlieus, out of which it may not stray the breadth of a hair upon peril of being lost."

The old Earl of Norwich, who was esteemed the greatest wit in Charles the First's reign, when Charles the Second came to the throne was thought nothing of.

THE TURKISH LANGUAGE.

The Turks, notwithstanding the conscientious moods of their language, are not more remarkable for veracity than their neighbours, who, in ancient times, made so much use of the indefinite tenses, and were said to be always liars.—*The Doctor.*

LORD THURLOW.

Charles Butler, in his "Reminiscences," thus mentions a speech of Lord Thurlow's in reply to an attack of the duke of Grafton, during the inquiry into Lord Sandwich's administration of Greenwich Hospital. "His grace's action and delivery, when he addressed the house, were singularly dignified and graceful; but his matter was not equal to his manner. He reproached Lord Thurlow with his plebeian extraction, and his recent admission into the peerage. Particular circumstances caused Lord Thurlow's reply to make a deep impression on the reminiscent. His lordship had spoken too often, and began to be heard with a civil but visible impatience. Under these circumstances, he was attacked in the manner we have mentioned. He rose from the woolsack, and advanced slowly to the place, from which the chancellor generally addresses the house; then, fixing on the duke the look of Jove, when he has grasped the thunder;—'I am amazed,' he said, in a level tone of voice, 'at the attack which the noble duke has made upon me. Yes, my lords,' considerably raising his voice, 'I am amazed at his grace's speech. The noble duke cannot look before him, behind him, or on either side of him, without seeing some noble peer, who owes his seat in this house to his successful exertions in this profession to which I belong. Does he not feel that it is as honourable to owe it to these, as to being the accident of an accident? To all these noble lords the language of the noble duke is as applicable and as insulting as it is to myself. But I do not fear to meet it single and alone. No one venerates the peerage more than I do,—but, my lords, I must say that the peerage solicited me, not I the peerage. Nay more,—I can say and will say, that as a peer of parliament,—as speaker of this right honourable house,—as keeper of the great seal,—as guardian of his majesty's conscience,—as Lord High Chancellor of England,—nay, even in that character alone, in which the noble duke would think it an affront to be considered,—but which character none can deny *me*,—as a MAN, I am at this moment as respectable,—I beg leave to add,—I am at this time as much respected as the proudest peer I now look down upon.' The effect of this speech, both within the walls of parliament and out of them, was prodigious. It gave Lord Thurlow an ascendency in the house, which no chancellor had ever possessed; it invested him, in public opinion, with a character of independence and honour; and this, although he was ever upon the unpopular side of politics, made him always popular with the people."

PICKPOCKET.

A gentleman, who saw Wilkes's carriage drawn by men, (the horses being taken off,) complained to the lord mayor that he had lost his handkerchief in the crowd. "Very possibly," said his lordship, "I fancy one of Wilkes's coach-horses has picked your pocket."

ALMANACS.

In the last century, when a countryman had walked to the nearest town, thirty miles distant, for the express purpose of seeing an almanac, the first that had been heard of in those parts, his inquiring neighbours crowded round the man on his return. "Well, well," said he, "I know not! it maffles and talks. But all I could make out is, that Collop Monday falls on a Tuesday next year."—*The Doctor.*

MATERIALISM.

Sydney Smith was once dining with a French gentleman, who was indulging, not, perhaps, in the best possible taste, both before and during dinner, in a variety of freethinking speculations, and ended by avowing himself a materialist. "Very good soup this," said Mr. Smith. "*Oui, Monsieur, c'est excellente.*" "Pray, sir, do you believe in a *cook?*"

SCHOOL RECOLLECTIONS.

With some persons the awes and terrors of youth last for ever and ever. I know, for instance, an old gentleman of sixty-eight, who said to me one morning at breakfast, with a very agitated countenance, "I dreamed last night that I was flogged by Dr. Raine." Fancy had carried him back five and fifty years in the course of that evening. Dr. Raine and his rod were just as awful to him in his heart, then, as they had been at thirteen.—*Thackeray.*

FOUR INGREDIENTS IN CONVERSATION.

The first ingredient in conversation is truth; the next, good sense; the third, humour; and the fourth, wit.—*Sir William Temple.*

ENGLISH—GERMAN.

An English lady resident at Coblentz, one day wishing to order of her German servant (who did not understand English) a boiled fowl for dinner, Grettel was summoned, and that experiment began. It was one of the lady's fancies, that the less her words resembled her native tongue, the more they must be like German. So her first attempt was to tell the maid that she wanted a cheeking, or keeking. The maid opened her eyes and mouth, and shook her head. "It's to cook," said the mistress, "to cook, to put in an iron thing, in a pit—pat—pot." "Ish understand risht," said the maid, in her Coblentz patois. "It's a thing to eat," said her mistress, "for dinner—for deener—with sauce, soace—sowose. What on earth am I to do?" exclaimed the lady in despair, but still making another attempt. "It's a little creature—a bird—a bard—a beard—a hen—a hone—a fowl—a fool; it's all covered with feathers—fathers—feeders!" "Ha, ha," cried the delighted German, at last getting hold of a catchword, "Ja, ja! fedders—ja woh!" and away went Grettel, and in half an hour returned triumphantly, with a bundle of stationers' quills.—*Hood.*

SYDNEY SMITH ON CANNING.

When Mr. Canning is jocular he is strong; when he is serious he is like Samson in a wig; any ordinary person is a match for him; a song, an ironical letter, a burlesque ode, a smart speech of twenty minutes, full of gross misrepresentations and clever turns, excellent language, a spirited manner, lucky quotation, success in provoking dull men, some half information picked up in Pall Mall in the morning; these are our friend's natural weapons; all these things he can do; here I allow him to be truly great; nay, I will be just, and go still farther, if he would confine himself to these things, and consider the *facetæ* and the playful to be the basis of his character, he would, for that species of man, be universally regarded as a person of a very good understanding; call him a legislator, a reasoner, and the conductor of the affairs of a great nation, and it seems to me as absurd as if a butterfly were to teach bees to make honey. That he is an extraordinary writer of small poetry, and a diner-out of the highest lustre, I do most readily admit. After George Selwyn, and perhaps Tickell, there has been no such man for this half century. The foreign secretary is a gentleman, a respectable as well as a highly agreeable man in private life; but you may as well feed me with decayed potatoes, as console me for the miseries of Ireland, by the resources of his *sense* and his *discretion*. It is only the public situation which this gentleman holds, which entitles me or induces me to say so much about him. He is a fly in amber; nobody cares about the fly: the only question is, How the devil did it get there? Nor do I attack him from the love of glory, but from the love of utility, as a burgomaster hunts a rat in a Dutch dyke, for fear it should flood a province.

PAYING FOR THINGS.

One cannot bear to pay for articles he used to get for nothing. When Adam laid out his first penny upon nonpareils at some stall in Mesopotamia, I think it went hard with him, reflecting upon his old goodly orchard, where he had so many for nothing.—*Lamb.*

GAIN OF A LOSS.

Montaigne has a pleasant story of a little boy, who, when his mother had lost a law-suit which he had always heard her speak of as a perpetual cause of trouble, ran up to her in great glee, to tell her of the loss, as a matter for congratulation and joy; the poor child thinking it was like losing a cough, or any other bodily ailment.

ODD PARALLEL.

It was a clumsy and cruel contrivance of the Romans, to use hedge-hogs for clothes-brushes, and prepare them for it by starving them to death; our method of sweeping chimneys is not more ingenious, and little less inhuman.—*Southey.*

AN INTERRUPTION.

It is not easy to put me out of countenance, or interrupt the feeling of the time, by mere external noise or circumstance; yet once I was thoroughly *done up*. I was reciting at a particular house, *the Remorse*, and was in the midst of Athadra's description of the death of her husband, when a scrubby boy with a shining face set in dirt, burst open the door, and cried out: "Please, ma'am, master says, will you ha', or will you *not* ha', the pin round?"—*Coleridge.*

SECRET HISTORY OF BOOKS.

If the secret history of books could be written, and the author's private thoughts and meanings noted down along-side of his story, how many insipid volumes would become interesting, and dull tales excite the reader.—*Thackeray.*

RELIGIOUS PERSECUTION.

Sydney Smith, in Peter Plymley's Letters, after showing the folly of oppressing the Irish Catholics, says, "I admit there is a vast luxury in selecting a particular set of Christians, and in worrying them as a boy worries a puppy-dog; it is an amusement in which all the young English are brought up from their earliest days. Cruelty and injustice must, of course, exist; but why connect them with danger? Why," he asks, "torture a bull-dog, when you can get a frog or a rabbit?"

UNANIMITY.

"We must be unanimous," said Hancock, on the occasion of signing the Declaration of Independence; "there must be no pulling different ways." "Yes," answered Franklin, "we must all hang together, or most assuredly we shall all *hang separately.*"

OFFICIAL DRESS.

The Americans, we believe, are the first persons who have discarded the tailor in the administration of justice, and his auxiliary the barber—two persons of endless importance in codes and pandects of Europe. A judge administers justice, without a calorific wig and party-coloured gown, in a coat and pantaloons. He is obeyed, however; and life and property are not badly protected in the United States. We shall be denounced by the laureate as atheists and jacobins; but we must say, that we have doubts whether one atom of useful influence is added to men in important situations by any colour, quantity, or configuration of cloth and hair. The true progress of refinement, we conceive, is to discard all the mountebank drapery of barbarous ages. One row of gold and fur falls off after another from the robe of power, and is picked up and worn by the parish beadle and the exhibitor of wild beasts. Meantime, the afflicted wiseacre mourns over equality of garment; and wotteth not of two men, whose doublets have cost alike, how one shall command and the other obey.—*Sydney Smith.*

PREACHING TO THE POOR.

A woman in humble life was asked one day, on her way back from church, whether she had understood the sermon,—a stranger having preached. "Wud I hae the presumption!" was her simple and contented answer.

"Well, Master Jackson," said his minister, walking homeward after service, with an industrious labourer, who was a constant attendant; "well, Master Jackson, Sunday must be a blessed day of rest for you, who work so hard all the week! And you make good use of the day; for you are always to be seen at church!" "Aye, sir," replied Jackson, "it is, indeed, a blessed day; I works hard enough all the week; and then I comes to church o' Sundays, and sets me down, and lays my legs up, and *thinks o' nothing*."—*The Doctor.*

SEARCH AFTER CONTENTMENT.

I know a man that had health and riches, and several houses, all ready furnished, and would often trouble himself and family to be moving from one house to another, and being asked by a friend why he removed so often from one house to another, replied, "It was to find content in some one of them." But his friend, knowing his temper, told him if he would find content in any one of his houses, he must leave himself behind him; for content will never dwell but in a meek and quiet soul.—*Walton's Angler.*

LABOUR OF IDLENESS.

"There is more fatigue," says Tom Brown, "and trouble in a lady than in the most laborious life: who would not rather drive a wheelbarrow with nuts about the streets, or cry brooms, than be Arsennus?" (a fine gentleman.) When Marshal Turenne died, it was asked what had occasioned his death; to which Prince Eugene replied, "By doing nothing."

OLD BEAUTIES.

Lady Ailesbury and Lady Stafford preserved their loveliness so long, that Walpole called them *Huckaback Beauties,* that never wear out.

HYPOCRISY OF A LORD CHANCELLOR.

When Lord Thurlow had, in 1788, first intrigued actively with the whigs and the Prince upon the Regency question, being apparently inclined to prevent his former colleague, and now competitor, from clutching that prize—suddenly discovering from one of the physicians the approaching convalescence of the royal patient, he at one moment's warning quitted the Carlton House party, with an assurance unknown to all besides, perhaps even to himself not known before, and in his place undertook the defence of the king's rights against his son and his partisans. The concluding sentence of this unheard of performance was calculated to set all belief at defiance, coming from the man and in the circum stances. It assumed, for the sake of greater impressiveness, the form of a prayer; though certainly it was not poured out in the notes of supplication, but rather rung forth in the sounds that weekly call men to the service: "And when I forget my sovereign, may my God forget me!" Whereupon Wilkes, seated upon the foot of the throne, and who had known him long and well, is reported to have said, somewhat coarsely, but not unhappily, it must be allowed, "Forget you? He'll see you d——d first." —*Brougham's Statesman.*

EVENINGS AT HOLLAND HOUSE.

In the Edinburgh Review is a glowing picture of the evenings at Holland House and of its admirable master, drawn by a favourite guest shortly after Lord Holland's death:—

"The time is coming when, perhaps, a few old men, the last survivors of our generation, will in vain seek, amidst new streets, and squares, and railway stations, for the site of that dwelling which was in their youth the favourite resort of wits and beauties —of painters and poets—of scholars, philosophers, and statesmen. They will then remember, with strange tenderness, many objects once familiar to them—the avenue and the terrace, the busts and the paintings; the carving, the grotesque gilding, and the enigmatical mottoes. With peculiar fondness they will recall that venerable chamber, in which all the ancient gravity of a college library was so singularly blended with all that female grace and wit could devise to embellish a drawing-room. They will recollect, not unmoved, those shelves loaded with the varied learning of many lands and many ages; those portraits in which were preserved the features of the best and wisest Englishmen of two generations. They will recollect how many men who have guided the politics of Europe—who have moved great assemblies by reason and eloquence—who have put life into bronze and canvas, or who have left to posterity things so written, that it shall not willingly let them die—were there mixed with all that was loveliest and gayest in the society of the most splendid of capitals. They will remember the singular character which belonged to that circle, in which every talent and accomplishment, every art and science, had its place. They will remember how the last debate was discussed in one corner, and the last comedy of Scribe in another; while Wilkie gazed with modest admiration on Reynold's Baretti; while Mackintosh turned over Thomas Aquinas to verify a quotation; while Talleyrand related his conversations with Barras at the Luxembourg, or his ride with Lannes over the field of Austerlitz. They will remember, above all, the grace—and the kindness, far more admirable than grace—with which the princely hospitality of that ancient mansion was dispensed. They will remember the venerable and benignant countenance, and the cordial voice of him who bid them welcome. They will remember that temper, which years of pain, of sickness, of lameness, of confinement, seemed only to make sweeter and sweeter; and that frank politeness, which at once relieved all the embarrassment of the youngest and the most timid writer or artist, who found himself for the first time among ambassadors and earls. They will remember that constant flow of conversation, so natural, so animated, so various, so rich with observation and anecdote; that wit which never gave a wound; that exquisite mimicry which ennobled, instead of degrading; that goodness of heart which appeared in every look and accent, and gave additional value to every talent and acquirement. They will remember, too, that he whose name they hold in reverence was not less distinguished by the inflexible uprightness of his political conduct, than by his loving disposition and winning manners. They will remember, that, in the last lines which he traced, he expressed his joy that he had done nothing unworthy of the friend of Fox and Grey; and they will have reason to feel similar joy, if, in looking back on many troubled years, they cannot accuse themselves of having done any thing unworthy of men who were distinguished by the friendship of Lord Holland."

RELIGIOUS INTOLERANCE.

For what a length of years was it attempted to compel the Scotch to change their religion: horse, foot, artillery, and armed prebendaries, were sent out after the Presbyterian parsons and their congregations; but to their astonishment and horror, they could not introduce the book of Common Prayer, nor prevent that metaphysical people from going to heaven their true way, instead of our true way. With a little oatmeal for food, and a little sulphur for friction, allaying cutaneous irritation with the one hand, and holding his Calvinistical creed in the other, Sawney ran away to his flinty hills, sung his psalm out of tune his own way, and listened to his sermon of two hours long, amid the rough and imposing melancholy of the tallest thistles. But Sawney brought up his unbreeched offspring in a cordial hatred of his oppressors; and Scotland was as much a part of the weakness of England then as Ireland is at this moment. The true and the only remedy was applied; the Scotch were suffered to worship God after their own tiresome manner, without pain, penalty, and privation. No lightnings descended from heaven; the country was not ruined; the world is not yet come to an end; the dignitaries, who foretold all these consequences, are utterly forgotten; and Scotland has ever since been an increasing source of strength to Great Britain.

PLAYING CARDS.

It is quite right that there should be a heavy duty on cards; not only on moral grounds; not only because they act on a social party like a torpedo, silencing the merry voice, and numbering the play of the features; not only to still the hunger of the public purse, which, reversing the qualities of Fortunatus, is always empty, however much you may put into it; but, also, because every pack of cards is a malicious libel on courts, and on the world, seeing that the trumpery with number one at the head is the best part of them; and that it gives kings and queens no other companions than knaves.—*Guesses at Truth.*

SIGN FOR A SCHOOL.

A widow-friend of Lamb, having opened a preparatory school for children at Camden Town, said to him, "I live so far from town I must have a sign, I think you call it, to show that I teach children." "Well," he replied, "you can have nothing better than '*The Murder of the Innocents.*' "

FRENCH LANGUAGE.

When some one was expatiating on the merits of the French language to Mr. Canning, he exclaimed: "Why, what on earth, sir, can be expected of a language, which has but one word for *liking* and *loving*, and puts a fine woman and a leg of mutton on a par: *J'aime Julie; j'aime un gigot!*"

PULPIT ELOQUENCE.

Pulpit discourses have insensibly dwindled from speaking to reading; a practice, of itself, sufficient to stifle every germ of eloquence. It is only by the fresh feelings of the heart, that mankind can be very powerfully affected. What can be more ludicrous, than an orator delivering stale indignation, and fervour of a week old; turning over whole pages of violent passions, written out in German text; reading the tropes and apostrophes into which he is hurried by the ardour of his mind; and so affected at a preconcerted line and page, that he is unable to proceed any farther!—*Sydney Smith.*

VOLUMINOUS TRIFLING.

Dr. Shaw, the naturalist, was one day showing to a friend two volumes written by a Dutchman, upon the wings of a butterfly, in the British Museum. "The dissertation is rather voluminous, perhaps you will think," said the Doctor, gravely, "but it is immensely important."—*The Doctor.*

A SHARP SET.

The sexton of Salisbury Cathedral, was telling Lamb, that eight persons had dined together upon the top of the spire; upon which he remarked, that "They must have been sharp set."

SMALL KNOWLEDGE.

A luckless undergraduate of Cambridge, being examined for his degree, and failing in every subject upon which he was tried, complained that he had not been questioned upon the things which he knew. Upon which, the examining master tore off about an inch of paper, and pushing it towards him, desired him to write upon that all he knew.

DEFINITION OF TIMBER.

Lord Caernarvon defined timber as an excrescence on the face of the earth, placed there by Providence, for the payment of debts.

PUNNING TRANSLATION.

Coleridge's motto, "*sermoni proprioria,*" was translated by Lamb, as "properer for a sermon."

NARROW MINDS.

Dr. Johnson describes a class of persons, who make a figure in the House of Commons, while they have minds as narrow as the neck of a vinegar cruet.

PARLIAMENTARY JOKES.

Of what use a story may be, even in the most serious debates, may be seen from the circulation of old *Joes* in Parliament, which are as current there as their current namesakes used to be in the city some threescore years ago. A jest, though it shall be as stale as last year's newspaper, and as flat as Lord Flounder's face, is sure to be received with laughter by the collective wisdom of the nation: nay, it is sometimes thrown out like a tub to the whale, or like a trail of carrion to draw off hounds from the scent.—*The Doctor.*

PLEASANT TIMES.

From the beginning of the century to the death of Lord Liverpool, was an awful period for those who had the misfortune to entertain liberal opinions, and who were too honest to sell them for the ermine of the judge, or the lawn of the prelate:—a long and hopeless career in your profession—the chuckling grin of noodles, the sarcastic leer of the genuine political rogue—prebendaries, deans, and bishops made over your head—reverend renegadoes advanced to the highest dignities of the Church, for helping to rivet the fetters of Catholic and Protestant Dissenters—and no more chance of a whig administration than of a thaw in Zembla—these were the penalties exacted for liberality of opinion at that period; and not only was there no pay, but there were many stripes.—*Sydney Smith.*

ROYAL SAYING.

Alphonsus, surnamed the Wise, king of Aragon, used to say, "That among so many things as are by men possessed or pursued in the course of their lives, all the rest are baubles, besides old wood to burn, old wine to drink, old friends to converse with, and old books to read."

ST. EVREMONT.

St. Evremont was a celebrated duellist. He had discovered a particular thrust, which was honoured with his name, and called *la botte de St. Evremont.* This brave was witty and capricious, and would accept or refuse a challenge according to the fancy of the moment. Some of his duels were remarkable.

One day at the Café Procope, at dinner-time, he saw a gentleman seated at a *barvaroise*, and he exclaimed, "That is a confounded bad dinner for a gentleman!" The stranger thus insulted insisted upon satisfaction, which was granted; when St. Foix was wounded. Notwithstanding his injury, he coolly said to his antagonist, "If you had killed me, sir, I still should have persisted in maintaining that a *barvaroise* is a confounded bad dinner." Another time he asked a gentleman, whose aroma was not of the most pleasant nature, "Why the devil he smelt so confoundedly?" The offended party sent a challenge, which he refused in the following terms: "Were you to kill me you would not smell the less, and were I to kill you, you would smell the more." One day, meeting a lawyer whose countenance did not please him, he walked up to him and whispered in his ear, "Sir, I have some business with you." The attorney, not understanding the drift of his speech, quietly named an hour when he would find him in his office. The meeting was, of course, most amusing, the expression of St. Foix being, "that he wanted to have an *affaire* with him," a term which is equally applicable to a duel and a legal transaction.—*Millingen's History of Duelling.*

HUMAN ABILITIES.

The abilities of a man must fall short upon one side or the other, "like too scanty a blanket when you are abed, if you pull it upon your shoulders, you leave your feet bare; if you thrust it down upon your feet, your shoulders are uncovered."

IMPERTINENCE OF AN OPINION.

Sydney Smith says, that it is always considered as a piece of impertinence in England, if a man of less than two or three thousand a year has any opinions at all upon important subjects.

TOO LATE.

Some men are always too late, and, therefore, accomplish, through life, nothing worth naming. If they promise to meet you at such an hour, they are never present till thirty minutes after. No matter how important the business, either to yourself or to him, he is just as tardy. If he takes a passage in the steamboat, he arrives just as the boat has left the wharf, and the cars have started a few moments before he arrives. His dinner has been waiting for him so long that the cook is out of patience, and half the time is obliged to set the table again. This course, the character we have described, always pursues. He is never in season, at church, at a place of business, at his meals, or in his bed. Persons of such habits we cannot but despise. Much rather would we have a man too early to see us, and always ready, even if he should carry out his principle to the extent of the good deacon, who, in following to the tomb the remains of a husband and father, hinted to the bereaved widow, that, at a proper time, he should be happy to marry her. The deacon was in season; for scarcely had the relatives and friends retired to the house, before the parson made the same proposition to the widow. "You are too late," said she, "the deacon spoke to me at the grave."

PUN OF HOOK.

Hook and one of his friends happened to come to a bridge, "Do you know who built this bridge," said he to Hook. "No, but if you go over you'll be tolled."

HENDERSON, THE ACTOR.

Henderson, the actor, was seldom known to be in a passion. When at Oxford, he was one day debating with a fellow-student, who not keeping his temper, threw a glass of wine in the actor's face, when Henderson took out his handkerchief, wiped his face and coolly said, "That, sir, was a digression; now for the argument."

ANECDOTES OF THE LATE JAMES SMITH,

(One of the Authors of the Rejected Addresses.)

The Law Quarterly Magazine informs us, that James Smith's *coup d'essai* in literature "was a hoax, in the shape of a series of letters to the editor of the *Gentleman's Magazine*, detailing some extraordinary antiquarian discoveries and facts in natural history, which the worthy Sylvanus Urban inserted without the least suspicion; and we understand that the members of the Antiquarian and Zoological Societies are still occasionally in the habit of appealing to them in corroboration of their theories."

In the same article we find many characteristic and humorous anecdotes of Smith, some of which we shall quote.

"One of James Smith's favourite anecdotes related to Colonel Greville. The colonel requested his young ally to call at his lodgings, and in the course of their first interview related the particulars of the most curious circumstance in his life. He was taken prisoner during the American war, along with three other officers of the same rank; one evening they were summoned into the presence of Washington, who announced to them that the conduct of their government, in condemning one of his officers to death, as a rebel, compelled him to make reprisals, and that, much to his regret, he was under the necessity of requiring them to cast lots, without delay, to decide which of them should be hanged. They were then bowed out, and returned to their quarters. Four slips of paper were put into a hat, and the shortest was drawn by Captain Asgill, who exclaimed, 'I knew how it would be; I never won so much as a hit at backgammon in my life.' As Greville told the story, he was selected to sit up with Captain Asgill, under the pretence of companionship, but in reality to prevent him from escaping, and leaving the honour amongst the remaining three. 'And what,' inquired Smith, 'did you say to comfort him?' 'Why, I remember saying to him, when they left us, *D—— it, old fellow, never mind;*' but it may be doubted (added Smith) whether he drew much comfort from the exhortation. Lady Asgill persuaded the French minister to interpose, and the captain was permitted to escape.

"The fame of the brothers, James and Horatio Smith, was confined to a limited circle, until the publication of *The Rejected Addresses.* James used to dwell with much pleasure on the criticism of a Leicestershire clergyman: 'I do not see why they (*the Addresses*) should have been rejected: I think some of them very good.' This, he would add, is almost as good as the avowal of the Irish bishop, that there were some things in *Gulliver's Travels* which he could not believe.

"Though never guilty of intemperance, James Smith was a martyr to the gout; and, independently of the difficulty he experienced in locomotion, he partook largely of the feeling avowed by his old friend Jekyll, who used to say that, if compelled to live in the country, he would have the drive before his house paved like the streets of London, and hire a hackney-coach to drive up and down all day long.

"He used to tell, with great glee, a story showing the general conviction of his dislike to ruralities. He was sitting in the library at a country-house, when a gentleman proposed a quiet stroll into the pleasure-grounds:—

'Stroll! why don't you see my gouty shoe?'

'Yes, I see that plain enough, and I wish I'd brought one too, but they're all out now.'

'Well, and what then?'

'What, then? why, my dear fellow, you don't mean to say that you have really got the gout? I thought you had only put on that shoe to get off being shown over the improvements.'

"James Smith was also in the habit of sending Lady Blessington occasional epigrams, complimentary scraps of verse, or punning notes, like the following:—

'The newspapers tell us that your new carriage is very highly varnished. This, I presume, means your wheeled-carriage. The merit of your personal carriage has always been to my mind, its absence from all varnish. The question requires that a jury should be *impanelled.*'

"Or this:—

'DEAR LADY BLESSINGTON:

'When you next see your American friend, have the goodness to accost him as follows,—

'In England rivers all are males—
For instance, Father Thames;
Whoever in Columbia sails,
Finds them ma'mselles or dames.

'Yes, there the softer sex presides,
Aquatic, I assure ye,
And Mrs. Sippy rolls her tides,
Responsive to Miss Souri.

'Your ladyship's faithful and devoted servant,

'JAMES SMITH.'

"His bachelorship is thus recorded in his niece's album—

'Should I seek Hymen's tie
As a poet I die,
Ye Benedicts mourn my distresses!
For what little fame
Is annexed to my name,
Is derived from *Rejected Addresses*.'

"His solitary state, however, certainly proceeded rather from too discursive than too limited an admiration of the sex, for to the latest hour of his life, he gave a marked preference to their society, and disliked a dinner-party composed exclusively of males.

"The following is among the best of his good things. A gentleman, with the same christian and surname, took lodgings in the same house. The consequence was, eternal confusion of calls and letters. Indeed, the postman had no alternative but to share the letters equally between the two. 'This is intolerable, sir,' said our friend, 'and you must quit.' 'Why am I to quit more than you?' 'Because you are James the Second—and must *abdicate*.'

"As lawyers, we are glad to be able to add, that he *had* an unfeigned respect for the profession.

"Smith was rather fond of a joke on his own branch of the profession; he always gave a peculiar emphasis to the line in his song, on the contradiction in names;

'Mr Makepeace was bred an attorney;'

and would frequently quote Goldsmith's lines on

Hickey, the associate of Burke and other distinguished contemporaries:—

'He cherished his friend, and he relished a bumper;
Yet one fault he had, and that was a thumper.
Then, what was his failing? come tell it, and burn ye.
He was, could he help it? a special attorney.

"The following playful colloquy in verse took place at a dinner-table between Sir George Rose and Smith, in allusion to Craven-street, Strand, where he resided:—

J. S.—'In Craven-street, Strand, ten attorneys find place,
And ten dark coal-barges are moored at its base:
Fly, Honesty, fly to some safer retreat,
For there's craft in the river, and craft in the street.'

Sir G. R.—'Why should Honesty fly to some safer retreat,
From attorneys and barges, od rot 'em?
For the lawyers are *just* at the top of the street,
And the barges are *just* at the bottom.'

"He had a keen relish for life, but he spoke calmly and indifferently about dying—as in the verses on revisiting Chigwell:—

'I fear not, Fate, thy pendant shears;
There are who pray for length of years,
To them, not me, allot 'em:
Life's cup is nectar at the brink,
Midway a palatable drink,
And wormwood at the bottom.'

"This is not quite reconcilable with a remark he once made to the writer, that if he could go back to any former period of his life, he would prefer going back to forty. He was about that age when he first came into celebrity.

"On the occasion of another visit to Chigwell he wrote thus:—

'World, in thy ever busy mart,
I've acted no unnoticed part.
Would I resume it? Oh, no!
Four acts are done—the jest grows stale,
The waning lamps burn dim and pale,
And reason asks—*cui bono?*'"

One of the happiest, and assuredly the most profitable of epigrams, that was ever made, was written by Smith. Happening to dine out one day, he met at table an old gentleman, very weak in the legs, but with a fine, noble-looking head; Smith wrote the following on a scrap of paper, and slipped it around to him:—

"That which supports the body's length,
In due proportion spread,
In you mounts upward, and your strength
All settles in your head."

He thought no more of it, until some time after he was surprised to learn that the old gentleman dying, had left him twelve hundred pounds by his will.

"But Mr. Smith's happiest effort," says Barham, "was inclosed in a short note to his friend Count D'Orsay:—

27 Craven-street, Monday, June 6.

"MY DEAR COUNT—Will you give me Gallic immortality by translating the subjoined into French.

Sincerely yours, &c.

PIUS ÆNEAS.

'Virgil, whose magic verse enthralls,—
And who in verse is greater?
By turns his wand'ring hero calls,
Now *pius*, and now *pater*.
But when prepared the worse to brave,
An action that must pain us,
Queen Dido meets him in the cave,
He dubs him DUX TROJANUS.
And well he changes thus the word
On that occasion, sure—
PIUS ÆNEAS were absurd,
And PATER *premature*.' "

CLEVER PUN.

An actor, named Priest, was playing at one of the principal theatres. Some one remarked, at the Garrick Club, that there were a great many men in the pit. "Probably clerks, who have taken Priest's orders," said Mr. Poole, one of the best punsters, as well as one of the cleverest comic satirists of the day.

WIT AND LEARNING.

Wit is often found united with great learning; three of the most learned men that have ever lived, have been three of the wittiest—Cervantes, Rabelais, Butler.

HUMOUR AND GENIUS.

Men of humour are, in some degree, men of genius: wits are rarely so, although a man of genius may, amongst other gifts, possess wit—as Shakspeare. —*Coleridge.*

PRISON RETIREMENT.

Since the benevolent Howard attacked our prisons, incarceration has become not only healthy, but elegant; and a county jail is precisely the place to which any pauper might wish to retire, to gratify his taste for magnificence as well as for comfort. Upon the same principle, there is some risk that transportation will be considered as one of the surest roads to honour and wealth; and that no felon will hear a verdict of "*not guilty*," without considering himself as cut off in the fairest career of prosperity.—*Sydney Smith.*

TREASON.

Horne Tooke, on being asked by a foreigner of distinction, how much treason an Englishman might venture to write, without being hanged, replied, that "he could not inform him just yet, but that he was trying."

BOOK MADNESS.

A collector of scarce books, was one day showing me his small but curious hoard. "Have you ever seen a copy of this book?" he asked, with every volume that he put into my hands; and when my reply was, that I had not, he always rejoined, with a look and tone of triumphant delight, "I should have been exceedingly sorry if you had!"—*The Doctor.*

ENGLISH FRENCH.

The author of Eothen, after relating his conversation with a Frenchman at Cairo, says: "These answers of mine, as given above, are not meant for specimens of mere French, but of that fine, terse, nervous, *Continental English,* with which I and my compatriots make our way through Europe. This language, by-the-bye, is one possessing great force and energy, and is not without its literature—a literature of the very highest order. Where will you find more sturdy specimens of downright honest and noble English, than in the Duke of Wellington's 'French' dispatches?"

PARASITES.

Nature descends down to infinite smallness. A great man has his parasites; and if you take a large buzzing blue-bottle fly, and look at it in a microscope, you may see twenty or thirty little ugly insects crawling about it, which, doubtless, think their fly to be the bluest, grandest, merriest, most important animal in the universe; and are convinced the world would be at an end if it ceased to buzz.—*Sydney Smith.*

CHARLES LAMB.

Lamb never affected any spurious gravity. Neither did he ever act the *Grand Senior.* He did not exact that common copy-book respect, which some asinine persons would fain command, on account of the mere length of their years; as if, forsooth, what is bad in itself, could be the better for keeping; as if intellects already *mothery*, got any thing but *grand-mothery* by lapse of time!—*Hood.*

VARIETIES OF THE HUMAN RACE.

Lady Mary Wortley Montague said, that during all her travels she had never met with but three kinds of persons, Men, Women, and *Herveys.* These were the earls of Bristol, a family noted for their eccentricity.

JOHN KEMBLE.

I always had a great liking, I may say, a sort of nondescript reverence, for John Kemble. What a quaint creature he was! I remember a party, in which he was discussing, in his measured manner after dinner, when the steward announced his carriage. He nodded, and went on. The announcement took place twice afterward; Kemble each time nodding his head a little more impatiently, but still going on. At last, and for the fourth time, the steward entered and said, "Mrs. Kemble says, sir, she has the rheuma*tise* and cannot stay." "Add *ism!*" dropped John, in a parenthesis, and proceeded quietly in his harangue.

Kemble would correct any body at any time, and in any place. Dear Charles Matthews—a true genius in his line, in my judgment—told me that he was once performing privately before the king. The king was very much pleased with the imitation of

Kemble, and said, "I liked Kemble very much. He was one of my earliest friends. I remember once he was talking, and found himself out of snuff. I offered him my box. He declined taking any—'He, a poor actor, could not put his fingers into a royal box.' I said, 'take some, pray; you will obl*ee*ge me!' Upon which Kemble replied, 'It would become your royal mouth better to say, oblige me;' and took a pinch."—*Coleridge's Table-Talk.*

INFLUENCE OF WOMEN.

Man is but a rough pebble, without the attrition received from contact with the gentler sex: it is wonderful how the ladies pumice a man down into a smoothness which occasions him to roll over and over with the rest of his species, jostling but not wounding his neighbours, as the waves of circumstances bring him into collision with them.—*Capt. Marryat.*

FRENCHMEN.

Coleridge says of the French, that they are like grains of gunpowder, each by itself smutty and contemptible; but mass them together, and they are terrible indeed.

SIR JAMES MACKINTOSH.

The first points of character which every body noticed in Mackintosh, were the total absence of envy, hatred, malice, and uncharitableness. He could not hate, he did not know how to set about it. The gall-bladder was omitted in his composition, and if he could have been persuaded into any scheme of revenging himself upon an enemy, I am sure (unless he had been narrowly watched) it would have ended in proclaiming the good qualities, and promoting the interests of his adversary.

Till subdued by age and illness, his conversation was more brilliant and instructive than that of any human being I ever had the good fortune to be acquainted with. His memory (vast and prodigious as it was) he so managed as to make it a source of pleasure and instruction, rather than that dreadful engine of colloquial oppression into which it is sometimes erected. He remembered things, words, thoughts, dates, and every thing that was wanted. His language was beautiful, and might have gone from the fireside to the press; but though his ideas were always clothed in beautiful language, the clothes were sometimes too big for the body, and common thoughts were dressed in better and larger apparel than they deserved. He certainly had this fault, but it was not one of frequent commission.

Sir James had a good deal of humour; and I remember, amongst many other examples of it, that he kept us for two or three hours in a roar of laughter, at a dinner-party at his own house, playing upon the simplicity of a Scotch cousin, who had mistaken me for my gallant synonym, the hero of Acre. I never saw a more perfect comedy, nor heard ridicule so long and so well sustained. Sir James had not only humour, but he had wit also; at least, new and sudden relations of ideas flashed across his mind in reasoning, and produced the same effect as wit, and would have been called wit, if a sense of their utility and importance had not often overpowered the admiration of novelty, and entitled them to the higher name of wisdom. Then the great thoughts and fine sayings of the great men of all ages were intimately present to his recollection, and came out dazzling and delighting in his conversation. Justness of thinking was a strong feature in his understanding; he had a head in which nonsense and error could hardly vegetate: it was a soil utterly unfit for them.

Curran, the master of the rolls, said to Mr. Grattan, "You would be the greatest man of your age, if you would buy a few yards of red tape, and tie up your bills and papers." This was the fault or misfortune of Sir James Mackintosh; he never knew the use of red tape, and was utterly unfit for the common business of life. That a guinea represented a quantity of shillings, and that it would barter for a quantity of cloth, he was well aware; but the accurate number of the baser coin, or the just measurement of the manufactured article to which he was entitled for his gold, he could never learn, and it was impossible to teach him. Hence his life was often an example of the ancient and melancholy struggle of genius, with the difficulties of existence.—*Sydney Smith.*

HAPPINESS.

If you cannot be happy in one way, be happy in

another; and this facility of disposition wants but little aid from philosophy, for health and good-humour are almost the whole affair. Many run about after felicity, like an absent man hunting for his hat, while it is on his head, or in his hand.—*Sharp.* These persons want nothing to make them the happiest people in the world but the knowledge that they are so.

A SHE FOOL.

Lord Burleigh, in a capital letter of advice to his son Robert Cecil, advises him never to "choose a base and uncomely creature altogether for wealth; for it will cause contempt in others, and loathing in thee. Neither make choice of a dwarf or a fool; for by the one thou shalt beget a race of pigmies; the other will be thy continual disgrace; and it will yirk thee to hear her talk. For thou shalt find it, to thy great grief, that there is nothing more fulsome than a *she fool.*"

LORD CHIEF JUSTICE HOLT.

When Holt was Lord Chief Justice, he committed some enthusiasts to prison. The next day, one Lacy, who was of the same persuasion, went to his house, and asked to speak to him. The porter answered, his lordship was not well, and could not be seen. Lacy insisted that he must see him, for he was sent to him by the Lord. When this message was delivered, he obtained admittance. "I come," said he, "from the Lord, commanding thee to grant a *noli prosequi* to his faithful servants, whom thou hast unjustly committed to prison." "Thou canst not, certainly, have come from the Lord," replied Holt; "for he would have sent thee to the Attorney-General, knowing very well that it is not in my power to grant thy demand. Therefore, thou art a false prophet; and thou shalt go and keep thy friends company in prison."

PEDANTRY.

As I take it, the word is not properly used: because pedantry is the too frequent or unseasonable obtruding our own knowledge in common discourse, and placing too great a value upon it; by which definition, men of the court, or of the army, may be as guilty of pedantry as a philosopher or a divine; and it is the same vice in women, when they are over copious upon the subject of their petticoats, or their fans, or their china.—*Swift.*

SLEEPING IN CHURCH.

Many stories have been related of Swift, tending to show his utter disregard of all decorum in matters of religion, and among the rest one that has obtained universal belief, and which deserves to be killed off. This is an absurd story of his having one day found no one present at morning service but himself and the clerk, Roger Coxe, and commencing, "Dearly beloved Roger, the Scripture moveth us in sundry places, to acknowledge and confess our manifold sins and wickedness;" and so proceeding through the service. The whole of this story is untrue, no such scene ever occurred. It seems to have been an invention of Lord Orrery to discredit the dean's respect for religion. Swift's nephew said he had seen it in an old jest-book printed about the year 1560; probably all the other stories of the same nature may be disposed of in a like manner.

The following extract, however, is from a sermon actually preached by Swift in the cathedral at Dublin, with the text from Acts xx. 9: "And there sat in the window a certain young man, named Eutychus, being fallen into a deep sleep; and while Paul was long preaching, he sunk down from sleep, and fell down from the third loft, and was taken up dead." Swift then proceeds to say, "I have chosen these words with a design, if possible, to disturb some part of this audience of half an hour's sleep, for the convenience and exercise whereof this place, at this season of the day, is very much celebrated.

"There is, indeed, one mortal disadvantage to which all preaching is subject; that those who by the wickedness of their lives stand in the greatest need have usually the smallest share; for either they are absent upon account of idleness, or spleen, or hatred to religion, or in order to doze away the intemperance of the week; or, if they do come, they are sure to employ their minds any other way than regarding or attending to the business of the place.

"The accident which happened to the young man in the text, hath not been sufficient to discourage his successors; but, because the preachers now in the world however they do exceed St. Paul in the art of setting men to sleep, do extremely fall short of him in the working of miracles; therefore men are become so cautious as to choose more safe and convenient stations and postures for taking their repose, without hazard of their persons; and upon the whole matter, choose rather to trust their destruction to a miracle, than their safety."

THE THEATRE.

There is something in the word *Playhouse* which seems so closely connected, in the minds of some people, with sin and Satan, that it stands in their vocabulary for every species of abomination. And yet why? Where is every feeling more roused in favor of virtue than at a good play? Where is goodness so feelingly, so enthusiastically learned? What so solemn as to see the excellent passions of the human heart called forth by a great actor, animated by a great poet? To hear Siddons repeat what Shakspeare wrote? To behold the child and his mother—the noble and the poor artisan—the monarch and his subjects—all ages and all ranks convulsed with one common passion—wrung with one common anguish, and, with loud sobs and cries, doing involuntary homage to the God that made their hearts! What wretched infatuation to interdict such amusements as these! What a blessing that mankind can be allured from sensual gratification, and find relaxation and pleasure in such pursuits!—*Sydney Smith.*

HINT TO AUTHORS.

If I might give a short hint to an impartial writer, it would be to tell him his fate. If he resolved to venture upon the dangerous precipice of telling unbiassed truth, let him proclaim war with mankind—neither to give nor to take quarter. If he tells the crimes of great men, they fall upon him with the iron hands of the law; if he tells them of virtues, when they have any, then the mob attacks him with slander. But if he regards truth, let him expect martyrdom on both sides, and then he may go on fearless; and this is the course I take myself.—*De Foe.*

SUCCESS IN LIFE.

Half the failures in life arise from pulling in one's horse as he is leaping.—*Guesses at Truth.*

FINE SPEAKING.

It is an admirable thing to see how some people will labour to find out terms that may obscure a plain sense, like a gentleman I know, who would never say the weather grew cold, but that winter began to salute us: I have no patience with such coxcombs.—*Lady Temple.*

VOLTAIRE.

M. de Saint Ange, translator of the Metamorphoses of Ovid, was noted for a certain languishing and mawkish air in his conversation and deportment; having been, like every other member of the literary world, to pay his respects to Voltaire, and being ambitious of concluding his visit with some stroke of genius, said, twirling his hat prettily between his thumbs: "I am only come to-day, sir, to see Homer; another day I shall come to see Euripides and Sophocles, afterward Tacitus, and then Lucian." "*Sir*," answered Homer, "*I am very old, could you not make all the visits at once?*"

I!

The proudest word in English, to judge of its way of carrying itself, is *I*. It is the least of monosyllables, if it be indeed a syllable: yet who in good society ever saw a little one. Indeed, this big one-lettered pronoun is quite peculiar to John Bull; as much so as Magna Charta, with which, perchance, it may not be altogether unconnected. At least, it certainly is an apt symbol of the national character, both in some of its nobler and of its harsher features. In it you may discern the Englishman's freedom, his unbending firmness, his straightforwardness, his individuality of character; you may also see his self-importance, his arrogance, his opinionativeness, his propensity to separate and seclude himself from his neighbours, and to look down on all mankind with contempt. Look at four Englishmen in a stage-coach: the odds are, they will be sitting as stiff and as unsociable as four *I's*.—*Guesses at Truth.*

THE ART OF HAPPINESS.

Sharp gives us the true method to be happy: "The chief secret of comfort, lies in not suffering trifles to vex one, and in prudently cultivating an undergrowth of small pleasures, since very few great ones, alas! are let on long leases."

USE AND ABUSE.

A certain authoress interdicts cards and assemblies. No cards, because cards are employed in gaming; no assemblies, because many dissipated persons pass their lives in assemblies. Carry this but a little further, and we must say, no wine, because of drunkenness; no meat, because of gluttony; no use, that there may be no abuse!—*Sydney Smith.*

THE MIDDLE STATION.

My father bade me observe it, and I should always find that the calamities of life were shared among the upper and lower part of mankind; but that the middle station had the fewest disasters, and was not exposed to so many vicissitudes as the higher or lower part of mankind; nay, they were not subject to so many distempers and uneasiness, either of body or mind, as those were who by vicious living, luxury, and extravagances, on one hand, or by hard labour, want of necessaries, and mean or insufficient diet, on the other hand, bring distempers upon themselves by the natural consequences of their way of living; that the middle station of life was calculated for all kind of virtues and all kind of enjoyments; that peace and plenty were the handmaids of a middle fortune; that temperance, moderation, quietness, health, society, all agreeable diversions, and desirable pleasures, were the blessings attending the middle station of life; that this way men went silently and smoothly through the world, and comfortably out of it, not embarrassed with the labours of the hand or the head, not sold to a life of slavery for daily bread, or harassed with perplexed circumstances, which rob the soul of peace, and the body of rest; nor enraged by the passion of envy, or the secret burning lust of ambition for great things; but in easy circumstances, sliding gently through the world, and sensibly tasting the sweets of living, without the bitter; feeling that they are happy, and learning by every day's experience to know it more sensibly.—*Robinson Crusoe.*

SIR WILLIAM TEMPLE AND LORD BROUNCKER.

Sir William Temple and Lord Brouncker, the President of the Royal Society, being neighbours in the country, had frequently very sharp contentions; like other great men, one would not bear an equal, and the other would not admit of a superior. Lord Brouncker was a great admirer of curiosities, of which he had a very good collection, which Sir William Temple used to undervalue on all occasions, disparaging every thing of his neighbour's, and giving his own things the preference. This by no means pleased his lordship, who took all opportunities of being revenged. One day, as they were discoursing together of their several rarities, Brouncker replied to him very seriously and gravely: "Sir William, say no more of the matter; you must at length yield to me, I having lately got something which it is impossible for you to obtain, for my Welsh steward has sent me a flock of geese; and these are what you can never have, since *all your geese are swans.*"

MISCELLANEOUS WRITING.

Peace be with the soul of that charitable and courteous author, who, for the common benefit of his fellow-authors, introduced the ingenious way of miscellaneous writing!—*Shaftesbury.*

CONVERSATION.

Conversation must and ought to grow out of materials on which men can agree, not upon subjects which try the passions.—*Sydney Smith.*

A companion that feasts the company with wit and mirth, and leaves out the sin which is usually mixed with them, he is the man; and let me tell you, good company and good discourse are the very sinews of virtue.—*Izaak Walton.*

Surely one of the best rules in conversation, is never to say a thing which any of the company can reasonably wish we had rather left unsaid.—*Swift.*

It is a secret known but to few, yet of no small use in the conduct of life, that when you fall into a man's conversation, the first thing that you should consider is, whether he has a greater inclination to hear you, or that you should hear him.—*Steele.*

Conversation is a traffic; and if you enter into it without some stock of knowledge to balance the account perpetually betwixt you, the trade drops at once.—*Sterne.*

The most necessary talent in a man of conversation, is a good judgment.—*Steele.*

The wit of conversation consists more in finding it in others, than in showing a great deal yourself; he who goes from your conversation pleased with himself and his own wit, is perfectly well pleased with you.—*La Bruyère.*

A general fault in conversation, is that of those who affect to talk of themselves. Some, without any ceremony, will run over the history of their lives; will relate the annals of their diseases, with the several symptoms and circumstances of them; will enumerate the hardships and injustice they have suffered in court, in parliament, in love, or in law. Others are more dexterous, and with great art will lie on the watch to hook in their own praise. They will call a witness to remember, they always foretold what would happen in such a case, but none would believe them; they advised such a man from the beginning, and told him the consequences, just as they happened, but he would have his own way. Others make a vanity of telling their faults; they are the strangest men in the world; they cannot dissemble; they own it is a folly; they have lost abundance of advantages by it; but if you would give them the world, they cannot help it; there is something in their nature that abhors insincerity and constraint; with many other insufferable topics of the same altitude.—*Swift.*

FLATTERING EPITAPHS.

Charles Lamb, when a little boy, walking in a church-yard with his sister, and reading the epitaphs, said to her, "Mary, where are all the naughty people buried?"

VOLUMINOUS AUTHORS.

There is an event recorded in the Bible, which men who write books, should keep constantly in their remembrance. It is there set forth, that many centuries ago, the earth was covered with a great flood, by which the whole of the human race, with the exception of one family, were destroyed. It appears, also, that from thence, a great alteration was made in the longevity of mankind, who, from a range of seven or eight hundred years, which they enjoyed before the flood, were confined to their present period of seventy or eighty years. This epoch in the history of man, gave birth to the two-fold division of the antediluvian and postdiluvian style of writing, the latter of which naturally contracted itself into those inferior limits which were better accommodated to the abridged duration of human life and literary labour. Now, to forget this event—to write without the fear of the deluge before his eyes, and to handle a subject as if mankind could lounge over a pamphlet for ten years, as before their submersion—is to be guilty of the most grievous error into which a writer can possibly fall.—*Sydney Smith.*

SIR HENRY WOTTON.

The following beautiful, but not enough known verses, were written by Sir Henry Wotton on his "dear mistress," Elizabeth, queen of Bohemia, daughter of James the First, and for whom he bore such an extraordinary respect as to give away a valuable diamond, presented to him by the emperor of Germany, because it "came from an enemy to his Royal Mistress, the queen of Bohemia."

"You meaner beauties of the night,
  That poorly satisfy our eyes
More by your number than your light,
  You common people of the skies;
  What are you when the sun shall rise?

You curious chanters of the wood,
  That warble forth dame Nature's lays,
Thinking your voices understood
  By your weak accents; what your praise,
  When Philomel her voice shall raise?

You violets that first appear,
  By your pure purple mantles known,
Like the proud virgins of the year,

As if the spring were all your own;
What are you when the rose is blown?

So when my mistress shall be seen,
In form and beauty of her mind,
By virtue first, then choice a Queen,
Tell me, if she were not designed
The eclipse and glory of her kind?"

ENGLISH AND FRENCH SUICIDES.

There is an absurd and ancient accusation against us, which ought, by this time, to be known by our accusers, the French, to be unfounded on fact, viz.: our *unequalled* propensity to suicide. That offence is far more frequent among the French themselves than with us. In the year 1816, the number of suicides committed in London amounted to seventy-two; in the same year, at Paris, they amounted to one hundred and eighty-eight, (not taking into account the number of unfortunates exposed at the Morgue,) the population of Paris being some 400,000 less than that of London! But suicides, if not unequalled in number by those of other countries, are indeed frequent with us, and so they always will be in countries where men can be reduced in a day from affluence to beggary. The loss of fortune is the general cause of the voluntary loss of life. Wounded pride,—disappointment,—the schemes of an existence laid in the dust,—the insulting pity of friends,—the humbled despair of all our dearest connections for whom perhaps we toiled and wrought,—the height from which we have fallen,—the impossibility of regaining what we have lost,—the searching curiosity of the public, —the petty annoyance added to the great woe,—all rushing upon a man's mind in the sudden convulsion and turbulence of its elements, what wonder that he welcomes the only escape from the abyss into which he has been hurled.

If the Spaniards rarely commit suicides, it is because they, neither a commercial nor gambling people, are not subject to such reverses. With the French it is mostly the hazard of dice, with the English, the chances of trade that are the causes of this melancholy crime—melancholy, for it really deserves that epithet with us. We do not set about it with the mirthful gusto which characterizes the *felo de se* in the Frenchman's native land. We have not yet among our numerous clubs, instituted a club of suicides, all sworn to be the happiest dogs possible, and not outlive the year! These gentlemen ask you to see them "go off," as if death were a place in the *malle poste*. "Will you dine with me to-morrow, my dear Dubois?"

"With the greatest pleasure; yet now I think of it, I am particularly engaged to shoot myself; I am really *au désespoir!* but one can't get off *such* an engagement you know."

"I would not ask such a thing, my dear fellow. Adieu! By the way if you ever come back to Paris again, I have changed my lodgings, *au plaisir!*"

Exeunt the two friends; the one twirling his moustaches, the other humming an opera tune.

This gayety of suicidalism, is not the death *à la mode* with us; neither are we so sentimental in these delicate matters, as our neighbours over the water. We do not shoot each other by way of being romantic. Ladies and gentlemen forced to "part company," do not betake themselves "to a retired spot," and tempt the dread unknown, by a brace of pistols, tied up with cherry-coloured ribbons.—*England and the English.*

ODDS AND ENDS.

A dinner of fragments is often said to be the best dinner. So are there few minds but might furnish some instruction and entertainment out of their scraps, their odds and ends of thoughts. They who cannot weave a uniform web, may at least produce a piece of patchwork.—*Guesses at Truth.*

TRUE RICHES.

Providence has decreed, that those common acquisitions—money, gems, plate, noble mansions, and dominion, should be sometimes bestowed on the indolent and unworthy; but those things which constitute our true riches, and which are properly our own, must be procured by our own labour.—*Erasmus.*

ENJOYING AND POSSESSING.

When I walk the streets, I use the following natural maxim, viz.: that he is the true possessor of a thing who enjoys it, and not he that owns it without the enjoyment of it, to convince myself that I have a property in the gay part of all the gilt chariots that I meet, which I regard as amusements designed to delight my eyes, and the imagination of those kind people who sit in them gayly attired only to please me. I have a real, and they only have an imaginary pleasure from their exterior embellishments. Upon the same principle, I have discovered that I am the natural proprietor of all the diamond necklaces, the crosses, stars, brocades, and embroidered clothes, which I see at a play or birthnight, as giving more natural delight to the spectator than to those that wear them. And I look on the beaux and ladies as so many paroquets in an aviary, or tulips in a garden, designed purely for my diversion. A gallery of pictures, a cabinet, or library, that I have free access to, I think my own. In a word, all that I desire is the use of things, let who will have the keeping of them. By which maxim, I am grown one of the richest men in Great Britain; with this difference, that I am not a prey to my own cares, or the envy of others.—*Berkeley.*

BUTTS.

A man is not qualified for a butt, who has not a good deal of wit and vivacity, even in the ridiculous side of his character. A stupid butt is only fit for the conversation of ordinary people—men of wit require one that will give them play, and bestir himself in the absurd part of his behaviour. A butt with these accomplishments frequently gets the laugh on his side, and turns the ridicule upon him that attacks him. Sir John Falstaff was a hero of this species, and gives a good description of himself, after the capacity of a butt, after the following manner: "Men of all sorts," says that merry knight, "take a pride to gird at me. The brain of man is not able to invent any thing that tends to laughter more than I invent, or is invented on me. I am not only witty in myself, but the cause that wit is in other men."—*Steele.*

SOURCE OF CONCEIT.

All affectation and display proceed from the supposition of possessing something better than the rest of the world possesses. Nobody is vain of possessing two legs and two arms; because that is the precise quantity of either sort of limb which every body possesses.—*Sydney Smith.*

GENTLEMAN.

A very expressive word in our language, a word denoting an assemblage of many real virtues, and a union of manners at once pleasing and commanding respect.—*Charles Butler.*

There exists in England, a *gentlemanly* character, a *gentlemanly* feeling, very different even from that which is the most like it—the character of a well-born Spaniard—and unexampled in the rest of Europe.—*Coleridge.*

The French, generally speaking, have the *gentlemanly manners* without the *gentlemanly spirit;* with the English, it is often the reverse, they have the *gentlemanly spirit,* without the *manners.*

HORRORS OF SEASICKNESS.

"Mind cannot conceive," says Matthews, in his very entertaining "Diary of an Invalid," after informing us of his state on board ship, "nor imagination paint the afflicted agonies of this state of suffering. I am surprised the poets have made no use of it in their descriptions of the place of torment; for it might have furnished an excellent hint for improving the punishment of their hells. What are the waters of Tantalus, or the stone of Sisyphus, when compared with the throes of seasickness?

"The depression and despondency of spirit which accompany this sickness, deprive the mind of all its energy, and fill up the last trait in the resemblance, by taking away even the consolations of hope—that last resource of the miserable—which comes to all, but the damned and the seasick."

EMPHATIC OATH.

Some time after the massacre of St. Bartholomew, the deputies sent by those of the reformed religion were treating with the king, the queen-mother, and some of the council for a peace. The articles were mutually agreed upon; and they were debating on what should be the security for the performance of these articles. After some particulars had been proposed and rejected, the queen-mother said, "Is not the word of a king sufficient security?" One of the deputies answered, "No, madam, by St. Bartholomew."

MEN AND BEASTS.

I should be very sorry to do injustice to the poor brutes, who have no professors to revenge their cause by lecturing on *our* faculties; and at the same time I know there is a very strong anthropological party, who view all eulogisms on the brute creation with a very considerable degree of suspicion, and look upon every compliment which is paid to the ape as high treason to the dignity of man.

There may, perhaps, be more of rashness and ill-fated security in my opinion, than of magnanimity or liberality; but I confess I feel myself so much at my ease about the superiority of mankind—I have such a marked and decided contempt for the understanding of every baboon I have yet seen—I feel so sure that the blue ape without a tail will never rival us in poetry, painting, and music, that I see no reason whatever why justice may not be done to the few fragments of soul and tatters of understanding which they may really possess. I have sometimes, perhaps, felt a little uneasy at Exeter 'Change, from contrasting the monkeys with the 'prentice-boys who are teazing them; but a few pages of Locke, or a few lines of Milton, have always restored me to tranquillity, and convinced me that the superiority of man had nothing to fear.—*Sydney Smith.*

POPE AND GARRICK.

Garrick's first theatrical appearance was in 1741, not long before the death of Pope, who was then in a weak and declining state. The poet had, however, the satisfaction of seeing him in one of his principal characters, and was boundless in his praise of the actor. "I am afraid that that young man will be spoiled," said he, "for he will never have a competitor."

Garrick gives the following interesting account of the occasion upon which Pope was present at the theatre, when he was to play the part of King Richard:

"When I was told that Pope was in the house, I instantaneously felt a palpitation at my heart; a tumultuous, not a disagreeable emotion in my mind. I was then in the prime of youth, and in the zenith of my theatrical ambition. It gave me particular pleasure that Richard was my character, when Pope was to see and hear me. As I opened my part, I saw our little poetical hero, dressed in black, seated in a side box near the stage, and viewing me with a serious and earnest attention. His look shot and thrilled, like lightning, through my frame; and I had some hesitation in proceeding, from anxiety and from joy. As RICHARD gradually blazed forth, the house was in a roar of applause, and the aspiring hand of POPE shadowed me with laurels."

OPPOSITE MINDS.

If black and white men live together, the consequence is, that unless great care be taken they quarrel and fight. There is nearly as strong a disposition in men of opposite minds to despise each other. A grave man cannot conceive what is the use of a wit in society; a person who takes a strong common-sense view of a subject, is for pushing out by the head and shoulders an ingenious theorist who catches at the lightest and faintest analogies; and another man, who scents the ridiculous from afar, will hold no commerce with him who tastes exquisitely the fine feelings of the heart, and is alive to nothing else; whereas talent is talent, and mind is mind, in all its branches! Wit gives to life one of its best flavours; common sense leads to immediate action, and gives society its daily motion; large and comprehensive views, its annual rotation; ridicule chastises folly and imprudence, and keeps men in their proper sphere; subtlety seizes hold of the fine threads of truth; analogy darts away to the most sublime discoveries; feeling paints all the exquisite passions of man's soul, and rewards him by a thousand inward visitations for the sorrows that come from without! God made it all! It is all good! We must despise no sort of talent: they all have their separate duties and uses; all the happiness of man for their object; they all improve, exalt, and gladden life.—*Sydney Smith.*

MASCULINENESS AND EFFEMINACY.

Men ought to be manly; women ought to be womanly or feminine. They are sometimes masculine, which men cannot be; but only men can be effeminate: for masculineness and effeminacy imply the palpable predominance in one sex, of that which is the peculiar characteristic of the other.—*Guesses at Truth.*

TALLEYRAND.

Talleyrand's sayings—his *mots*, as the French have it—are renowned; but these, alone, convey an imperfect idea of his whole conversation. They show, indeed, the powers of his wit, and the felicity of his concise diction; and they have a peculiarity of style, such that, if shown without a name, no one could be at a loss to whom he should attribute them. But they are far enough from showing the style of his conversation to those who have never heard it. A gentleman in company was one day making a somewhat zealous eulogy of his mother's beauty, dwelling on the topic at uncalled-for length—he himself having, certainly, inherited no portion of that kind under the marriage of his parents. "C'était, donc, monsieur votre père qui apparemment n'était pas trop bien," was the remark which at once released the circle from the subject. When Madame de Staël published her celebrated novel of *Delphine*, she was supposed to have painted herself in the person of the heroine, and M. Talleyrand in that of an elderly lady, who is one of the principal characters. "On me dit, (said he, the first time he met her,) que nous sommes tous les deux dans votre roman déguisés en femme." Rubhières, the celebrated author of the work on the Polish Revolution, having said, "Je n'ai fait qu'un méchanceté de ma vie." "Et quand finira-t-elle?" was M. Talleyrand's reply. "Genève est ennuyeuse, n'est-ce pas?" asked a friend. "Surtout quand on s'y amuse," was the answer. "Elle est insupportable," (said he, with a marked emphasis, of one well known; but as if he had gone too far, and to take something off of what he laid on, he added,) "Elle n'a que ce défaut-là." "Ah, je sens les tourmens d'enfer," said a person, whose life had been supposed to be somewhat of the loosest. "Déjà?" was the inquiry suggested by M. Talleyrand.—*Brougham.*

There is an anecdote recorded of Talleyrand, which shows that he not only could say witty things, but also could do them. Upon Charles the Tenth's death, he drove for a few days about Paris, carrying a piece of crape in his pocket; when he came by the neighbourhood of the Carlists, the crape was taken out and tied around his hat, and when he arrived at the quarter of the Tuilleries, he again slipped off the crape, and put it in his pocket.

STORY-TELLING.

I would advise all professors of the art of story-telling, never to tell stories but as they seem to grow out of the subject-matter of the conversation, or as they serve to illustrate, or enliven it. Stories that are very common, are generally irksome; but may be aptly introduced, provided they be only hinted at, and mentioned by way of allusion. Those that are altogether new, should never be ushered in, without a short and pertinent character of the chief persons concerned, because, by that means, you may make the company acquainted with them; and it is a certain rule, that slight and trivial accounts of those who are familiar to us, administer more mirth than the brightest points of wit in unknown characters. A little circumstance in the complexion or dress of the man you are talking of, sets his image before the hearer, if it be chosen aptly for the story.—*Steele.*

LIFE.

Democritus was a wiser man than Heraclitus. Those are the wisest, and the happiest, who can pass through life as a play; who, without making a farce of it, and turning every thing into ridicule, consider the whole period from the cradle to the coffin, as a well-bred comedy; and maintain a cheerful smile to the very last scene. For what is happiness but a Will-o'-the-wisp—a delusion—a terra-incognita—in pursuit of which thousands are tempted out of the harbour of tranquillity, to be tossed about, the sport of the winds of passion and the waves of disappointment, to be wrecked perhaps at last on the rocks of despair; unless they be provided with the sheet-anchor of religion—the only anchor that will hold in all weathers. This is a very stupid allegory, but it was preached to me this morning by a beautiful piece of sculpture which I saw. A female figure of Hope has laid aside her anchor, and is feeding a monstrous chimæra. The care and solicitude of Hope in tending this frightful creature, are most happily expressed; and the general effect is so touching, that it illustrates Shakspeare's phrase of *sermons in stones* with great felicity.—*Matthews.*

ROGUES.

Few people think better of others than of themselves, nor do they readily allow the existence of any virtue of which they perceive no traces in their own minds; for which reason it is next to impossible to persuade a rogue that you are an honest man; nor would you ever succeed by the strongest evidence, was it not for the comfortable conclusion which the rogue draws, that he who proves himself honest, proves himself a fool at the same time.—*Fielding.*

INDUSTRY.

It is better to wear out than to rust out.—*Cumberland.* We must not only strike the iron while it is hot, but strike it till "it is made hot."—*Sharp.*

"WHAT'S IN A NAME."

There are not a few of the best and most humane Englishmen of the present day, who, when under the influence of fear or anger, would think it no great crime to put to death people whose names begin with O or Mac. The violent death of Smith, Green, or Thomson, would throw the neighbourhood into convulsions, and the regular forms would be adhered to—but little would be really thought of the death of any body called O'Dogherty or O'Toole.—*Sydney Smith.*

COOKERY AND ASTRONOMY.

M. Henrion de Pensey, president of the Court of Cassation, expressed himself as follows, to three of the most distinguished men of science of their day: "I regard the discovery of a dish as a far more interesting event than the discovery of a star, for we have always stars enough, but we can never have too many dishes; and I shall not regard the sciences as sufficiently honoured or adequately represented, until I see a cook in the first class of the Institute."

NAPOLEON.

The most remarkable feature in the character of this strange being is his inconsistency; displaying as he does, at different times, the most opposite extremes of great and little—magnificence and meanness. This inconsistency, however, is sufficiently explained by his utter want of fixed principles of right and wrong. What can be expected of him who laughs at religion, and does not even possess a sense of honour to keep him steady in the path of greatness? Selfishness seems to have been the foundation of his system, the only principle which he acknowledged; and this will reconcile all the apparent inconsistencies of his conduct. Every thing was right to him that conduced to his own interest, by any means, however wrong; and as his mind seems to have had the power of expanding with his situation, so it had an equal power of contracting again; and he could at once descend from the elevation of his throne, to the pettiest considerations connected with his altered condition, accommodating himself in a moment, to all the variations of fortune. In a word, he was the Garrick of the great stage of the world, who could play in the Imperial Tragedy—carrying terror and pity into all bosoms—and reappearing in the part of Scrub, in the after-piece, with equal truth and fidelity of representation. We might admire the equanimity of such a temperament, if we did not find it associated with such a selfish and exclusive attention to his own personal safety, as robs it of all claims to our applause. After all, he is a truly extraordinary being—a wonderful creature, furnishing the most curious subject for examination to those who, abstractedly from all the national and political feelings of the present time, can consider him merely as a singular phenomenon, an anomalous variety in the strange history of human nature.—*Matthews.*

NARROW-MINDED PERSONS.

A narrow-minded person has not a thought beyond the little sphere of his own vision. "The snail," say the Hindoos, "sees nothing but his own shell, and thinks it the grandest palace in the universe."—*Sydney Smith.*

COLERIDGE'S NOTES IN BOOKS.

It was the custom of Coleridge whenever he read a book, to write down any thought, &c., which might occur to him while thus engaged, no matter to whom the volume might belong, or whether it was bound; and he appears to have deposited on their margins and blank leaves, "as in a confessional, the deepest, lightest, strangest, and, alas! saddest of his mental workings."

Some of these notes are curious; in one of the books which he had borrowed from Charles Lamb, (a copy of Donne's poems,) he writes as follows: "I shall die soon, my dear Charles Lamb, and then you will not be angry that I have bescribbled your book.—S. T. C., 2d May, 1811."

His friend alludes to this practice, in one of the most delightful of his essays, "The Two Races of Men:"—"To lose a volume to Coleridge," says Lamb, "carries some sense and meaning in it. You are sure that he will make one hearty meal on your viands, if he can give you no account of the platter after it. . . . . . . Reader, if haply thou art blessed with a moderate collection, be shy of showing it; or if thy heart overfloweth to lend them, lend thy books, but let it be to such a one as S. T. C.—he will return them (generally anticipating the time appointed) with usury; enriched with annotations, tripling their value. I have had experience. Many are these precious MMS. of his, (in *matter* oftentimes, and almost in *quantity*, not unfrequently vying with the originals,) in no very clerkly hand, legible in my Daniel; in old Burton; in Sir Thomas Browne; and those abtruser cogitations of the Greville, now, alas! wandering in Pagan lands."

VOLTAIRE'S SEAL-BOOK.

Voltaire was in the habit of keeping a book in which he pasted the seals of all his correspondents, and underneath each wrote the address of the person whose it happened to be. Whenever he received a letter, he would examine and ascertain from whence it came, by referring to his book; and if it came from a quarter he did not like, he replaced it in another envelope, and returned it unopened to the writer.

SERVANTS.

"This class of persons," says Ude, "assimilate no little to cats, enjoying what they can pilfer, but very difficult to please in what is given to them."

EXAGGERATION.

The passion of laughter, the strongest effect of ludicrous impressions, seems to be produced by the intensity, or more properly the excess of pleasurable ideas: *circum praecordia ludere*, is the proper character of this class of emotions. Thus a certain degree of fullness improves the figure, but if it be so increased to excessive fatness, it becomes risible. So, in the qualities of the mind, modesty is agreeable—extreme bashfulness is ridiculous: we are amused with vivacity—we laugh at levity. If we observe the conversation of a professed jester, *it will appear that his great secret consists in exaggeration.* This is also the art of caricaturists; add but a trifling degree of length or breadth to the features of an agreeable face, and they become ludicrous. In a like manner, unbolster Falstaff, and his wit will affect us less, the nearer he approaches to the size of a reasonable man.—*Ferriar.*

ITALIAN DINNER.

Matthews thus describes a dinner in Italy at which he was present: "Dined to-day with an Italian family, to whom I had brought letters of recommendation from Rome. This was the first occasion that I have had of seeing an Italian dress dinner; but there was scarcely any thing strange to excite remark. The luxury of the rich is nearly the same throughout Europe. Some trifling peculiarities struck me, though I think the deviations from our own customs were all improvements. There was no formal top and bottom to the table, which was round, and the host could not be determined from his place. All the dishes were removed from the table as they were wanted, carved by a servant at the sideboard and handed round. Each person was provided with a bottle of wine and a bottle of water, as with a plate and knife and fork. There was no asking to drink wine, nor drinking of healths, no inviting to eat nor carving for them. All these duties devolved on the domestics; and the conversation, which, in England, as long as the dinner lasts, is often confined to the business of eating, with all its important auxiliaries of sauces and seasonings, took its free course, unchecked by any interruptions arising out of the business in hand. This is surely the perfection of comfort—to be able to eat and drink what you please without exciting attention or remark—and I cannot but think it would be a great improvement upon our troublesome fashion of *passing the bottle*, to substitute the Italian mode of placing a separate decanter to each person."

LORD NORTH.

Lord North's wit was never surpassed, and it was attended with this singular quality, that it never gave offence, and the object of it was sure to join with pleasure in the laugh. The assault of Mr. Adam on Mr. Fox, and of Colonel Fullarton on Lord Shelburne, had once put the house into the worst possible humour, and there was more or less of savageness in every thing that was said. Lord North deprecated the too great readiness to take offence, which then seemed to possess the house. "One member," he said, "who spoke of me, called me, 'that thing called a minister;' to be sure," he said, patting his large form, "I am a thing; the member, therefore, when he called me a thing, said what was true; and I could not be angry with him; but, when he added, that thing called a minister, he called me the thing, which of all things, he himself wished most to be; and, therefore," said Lord North, "I took it as a compliment." These good-natured sallies dropped from him incessantly.—*Charles Butler.*

JOHN BULL.

There is nothing which an Englishman enjoys more than the pleasure of sulkiness—of not being forced to hear a word from any body which may occasion to him the necessity of replying. It is not so much that Mr. Bull disdains to talk, as that Mr. Bull has nothing to say. His forefathers have been out of spirits for six or seven hundred years, and seeing nothing but fog and vapour he is out of spirits too; and when there is no selling or buying, or no business to settle, he prefers being alone and looking at the fire. If any gentleman was in distress, he would lend a helping hand; but he thinks it no part of good neighbourhood to talk to a person because he happens to be near him. In short, with many excellent qualities, it must be acknowledged that the English are the most disagreeable of the nations of Europe—more surly and morose, with less disposition to please, to exert themselves for the good of society, to make small sacrifices, and to put themselves out of their way. They are content with Magna Charta and trial by jury; and think they are not bound to excel the rest of the world in small behaviour, if they are superior to them in great institutions.—*Sydney Smith.*

A COLD.

"Do you know what it is," asked Lamb of Bernard Barton, describing his own state, "to succumb under an insurmountable *daymare*—'a whoreson lethargy,' Falstaff calls it—an indisposition to do any thing, or to be any thing—a total deadness and distaste—a suspension of vitality—an indifference to locality—a numb soporifical good-for-nothingness—an ossification all over—an oysterlike indifference to passing events—a mind-stupor—a brawny defiance to the needles of a thrusting-in conscience—with a total irresolution to submit to water-gruel processes?"

"SIXTY YEARS SINCE."

The late Mr. Huddlestone, an amiable and accomplished gentleman, believed himself to be lineally descended from Athelstane, and consequently entitled to take precedence of all, including the proudest nobles, who did not equally partake of the blood-royal of the heptarchy. Some of this excellent person's evidences bore a strong resemblance to those of the Scotchman, who, in proof of his own descent from the Admirable Crichton, was wont to produce an ancient shirt marked A. C. in the tail, preserved, he said, as an heir-loom by the family; but Mr. Huddlestone's pedigree was admitted, and *Huddlestone* allowed to be an undeniable corruption of *Athelstane* by many of the distinguished amateur readers of Gwyllim; amongst others by the late Duke of Norfolk, who was sufficiently tenacious on such points. These two originals often met over a bottle to discuss the respective pretensions of their pedigrees, and on one of these occasions, when Mr. Huddlestone was dining with the duke, the discussion was prolonged till the descendant of the Saxon kings, fairly rolled from his chair upon the floor. One of the younger members of the family hastened, by the duke's desire, to re-establish him, but he sturdily repelled the proffered hand of the cadet—"Never," he hiccuped out, "shall it be said that the head of the house of Huddlestone was lifted from the ground by a younger branch of the house of Howard." "Well, then, my good old friend," said the good-natured duke, "I must try what I can do for you myself. The head of the house of Howard is too drunk to pick up the head of the house of Huddlestone, but he will lie down beside him with all the pleasure in the world:" so saying, the duke also took his place upon the floor. The concluding part of this anecdote has been plagiarized and applied to other people; but the authenticity of our version may be relied upon.—*Quarterly Review.*

FLEAS.

Except at Jerusalem, never think of attempting to go to sleep in a "holy city." Old Jews from all parts of the world go to lay their bones upon the sacred soil, and as these people never return to their homes, it follows that any domestic vermin which they may bring with them are likely to become permanently resident, so that the population is continually increasing. No recent census had been taken when I was at Tiberias, but I know that the congregation of fleas which attended at my church alone, must have been something enormous. It was a carnal, self-seeking congregation, wholly inattentive to the service which was going on, and devoted to the one object, of having my blood. The fleas of all nations were there. The smug, steady, importunate flea from Holywell-street; the pert, jumping "puce," from hungry France; the wary, watchful "pulce," with his poisoned stiletto; the vengeful "pulga," of Castile, with his ugly knife; the German "floh," with his knife and fork—insatiate—not rising from table; whole swarms from all the Russias, and Asiatic hordes unnumbered: all these were there, and all rejoiced in one great international feast. I could no more defend myself against my enemies, than if I had been "pain à discrétion," in the hands of a French patriot.—*Eothen.*

THE PENITENTS.

At Padre Caravita's, during Lent, the friars dress in sackcloth, trimmed with ashes; lights are put out, and every penitent, credits himself to heaven some dozen lashes, (the walls and pillars getting all the slashes,) the flogger setting up a pious moan, at every item of the bill he cashes; still working desperately at the stone, but giving not a touch to his own flesh and bone. One evening, as they sung their "miserere," with half the city listening at the door, (I think this famous chorus dull and dreary,) was heard a yell within, 'twas soon a roar, then a pitched battle on the holy floor; screams to the Virgin, howls to every saint! All thought the Fiend had come to claim his score; the men began to fly, the sex to faint. And still the battle raged, the howls came thicker; matters seemed looking black for "Church and State." Up marched the pursy guards of Rome's "Grand Vicar," heroes not much inclined to tempt their fate, for not a soul of them would touch the gate. At last, out burst the penitents *all whipped*, roaring at this new payment of "Church Rate." The truth transpired—an Englishman, equipped in cowl and gown, through the padre's door had slipped. He waited till the holy farce began; all stripped, all dark; not even a taper's smoke: then, marking a fat friar for his man, and taking a stout horsewhip from his cloak, on his broad back he laid a hearty stroke! the victim shrieked, as if he felt a sabre; John Bull amazingly enjoyed the joke, proceeding all the mummers to belabour, while each revenged the stripes upon his naked neighbour!—*The Modern Orlando.*

PLEASURES OF OLD AGE.

One forenoon I did prevail with my mother, to let them carry her to a considerable distance from the house, to a sheltered, sunny spot, whereunto we did often resort, formerly to hear the wood-pigeons which frequented the fir-trees thereabouts. We seated ourselves and did pass an hour or two very pleasantly. She remarked how merciful it was ordered, that these pleasures should remain to the last days of life; that when the infirmities of age make the company of others burdensome to us, and ourselves a burden to them, the quiet contemplation of the works of God affords a simple pleasure which needeth naught else than a contented mind to enjoy; the singing of birds, even a single flower, or a pretty spot like this, with its bank of primroses, and the brook running in there below, and this warm sunshine, how pleasant they are. They take back our thoughts to our youth, which age doth love to look back upon.—*Diary of Lady Willoughby.*

FRIGHTFUL TO THINK OF.

An injudicious adherent of Mr. Percival, the colleague of Canning, having mentioned drugs among the articles to be intercepted by the English ships, in order to make the French more disposed for peace, the opportunity which it offered to Sydney Smith for displaying his powers of ridicule, was too tempting to be lost, and he has thus "shown up" the affair, in the "Letters of Peter Plymley:"

"What a sublime thought," exclaims Peter, "that no purge can now be taken between the Weser and the Garonne; that the bustling pestle is still, the canorous mortar mute, and the bowels of mankind locked up for fourteen degrees of latitude! When, I should be curious to know, were all the powers of crudity and flatulence fully explained to his majesty's ministers? At what period was this great plan of conquest and constipation fully developed? In whose mind was the idea of destroying the pride and the plasters of France first engendered? Without castor oil they might, for some months, to be sure, have carried on a lingering war; but can they do without bark? Will the people live under a government where antimonial powders cannot be procured? Will they bear the loss of mercury? 'There's the rub.' Depend upon it, the absence of materia medica will soon bring them to their senses, and the cry of *Bourbon and bolus* burst forth from the Baltic to the Mediterranean."

VOLTAIRE'S PHYSIOGNOMY.

Voltaire's physiognomy, which is said to have been a combination of the eagle and the monkey, was illustrative of the character of his mind. If the soaring wing and piercing eye of the eagle opened to him all the regions of knowledge, it was only to collect materials for the gratification of that apish disposition, which seems to have delighted in grinning, with a malicious spirit of mockery, at the detected weaknesses and infirmities of human nature. Though a man may often rise the wiser, yet I believe none ever rose the *better* from the perusal of Voltaire.—*Matthews.*

NECESSITIES.

Mr. Wellesley Pole used to say, that it was impossible to live like a gentleman in England, under forty thousand a year; and Mr. Brummel told a lady who asked him, how much she ought to allow her son for dress, that it might be done for £800 a year *with strict economy.* Mr. Senior, in an excellent Essay on Political Economy recently published in the Encyclopædia Metropolitana, states that a carriage for a woman of fashion must be regarded as one of the necessaries of life, and we presume he would be equally imperative in demanding a cabriolet for a man.—*Quarterly Review.*

GIL BLAS.

At a house of great distinction, ten gentleman of taste were desired to frame, each of them, a list of the ten most entertaining works, which they had read. One work only found its way into every list—*Gil Blas.*

Campbell the poet, once said that he would rather have written Gil Blas than any of the Waverly Novels.

A CHANGER OF DYNASTIES.

In the third year of his present majesty, and in the 30th of his own age, Mr. Isaac Hawkins Brown, then upon his travels, danced one evening at the court of Naples. His dress was a volcanic silk with lava buttons. Whether (as the Neapolitan wits said) he had studied dancing under St. Vitus, or whether David, dancing in a linen vest, was his model, is not known; but Mr. Brown danced with such inconceivable alacrity and vigour, that he threw the queen of Naples into convulsions of laughter, which terminated in a miscarriage, and changed the dynasty of the Neapolitan throne.—*Sydney Smith.*

ABSENT-MINDEDNESS.

La Fontaine having attended the funeral of a friend, was so absent-minded as to call upon him a short time afterward. Being reminded of the fact, he was at first greatly surprised, but recollecting himself, said: "It is true enough, for I was there."

A NEW LIGHT.

Men of genius are rarely much annoyed by the company of vulgar people, because they have a power of looking *at* such persons as objects of amusement, of another race altogether.—*Coleridge.*

SCOTCH AND IRISH.

When George IV. went to Ireland, one of the "pisintry," delighted with his affability to the crowd on landing, said to the toll-keeper as the king passed through, "Och now! and his Majesty, God bless him, never does." "We lets 'em go free," was the answer. "Then there's the dirty money for ye," says Pat. "It shall never be said that the king came here, and found nobody to pay the turnpike for him." Moore, on his visit to Abbotsford, told this story to Sir Walter, when they were comparing notes as to the two royal visits. "Now, Mr. Moore," replied Scott, "there ye have just the advantage of us; there was no want of enthusiasm here; the Scotch folk would have done any thing in the world for his Majesty, but—pay the turnpike."

CHANGING HATS

Barry, the painter, was with Nollekens, at Rome, in 1760, and they were extremely intimate. Barry took the liberty one night, when they were about to leave the English coffee-house, to exchange hats with him; Barry's being edged with lace, and Nollekens' a very shabby plain one. Upon his returning the hat the next morning, he was requested by his friend, to let him know why he left him his gold-laced hat. "Why, to tell you the truth, my dear Joey," answered Barry, "I fully expected assassination last night, and I was to have been known by my laced hat." Nollekens often used to relate the story, adding, "It's what the Old Bailey people would call a true bill against Jem."

ENNUI AND TRAVEL.

If a man and an Englishman be not born of his mother with a natural Chiffney-bit in his mouth, there comes to him a time for loathing the wearisome ways of society—a time for not dancing quadrilles—

not sitting in pews—a time for pretending that Milton, and Shelley, and all sorts of mere dead people, were greater in death than the first living Lord of the Treasury—a time for scoffing and railing—for speaking lightly of the very opera, and all our most cherished institutions. It is from nineteen to two or three and twenty perhaps, that this war of man against men is like to be waged most sullenly. . . . . . The downs and moors of England can hold you no longer; with larger stride you burst away from these slips and patches of free land—you tread your path through the crowds of Europe, and at last on the banks of the Jordan, you joyfully know that you are upon the very frontier of all accustomed respectabilities. A little while you are free, and unlabelled, like the ground you compass; but civilization is coming and coming; you and your much-loved waste lands will be inclosed, and, sooner or later, you will be brought down to a state of utter usefulness.—*Eothen.*

JOHN WILKES.

Wilkes himself, in his soberer years, used to laugh pleasantly enough at the folly of his former dupes. One day, in his latter life, he went to court, and was asked by George III., in a good-humoured tone of banter, "how his friend, Serjeant Glynn was." This man had been one of his most furious partisans. "Pray, sir," replied Wilkes with affected gravity, "don't call Serjeant Glynn a friend of mine, *the fellow was a Wilkite, which your majesty knows I never was.*"

Brougham relates an anecdote of Wilkes, characteristic of this celebrated demagogue. Colonel Luttrell and he were standing on the Brentford hustings, when he asked his adversary privately, whether he thought there were more fools or rogues among the multitude of Wilkites spread out before them. "I'll tell them what you say, and put an end to you," said the Colonel; but perceiving the threat gave Wilkes no alarm, he added, "surely you don't mean to say you could stand here one hour after I did so?" "Why," answered the other, "*you* would not be alive one instant after." "How so?" "I should merely say it was a fabrication, and they would destroy you in the twinkling of an eye!"

TESTS.

We remember a remark of the late Earl of Dudley, to the effect that good melted butter is an unerring test of the moral qualities of your host. A distinguished connoisseur, still spared to the world, contends that the moral qualities of your hostess may in a like manner be tested by the potatoes, and he assures us that he was never known to re-enter a house where a badly dressed potato had been seen. The importance attached by another equally unimpeachable authority to the point, is sufficiently shown by what took place a short time since at the meeting of a club-committee specially called for the selection of a cook. The candidates were an Englishman from the Albion Club, and a Frenchman recommended by Ude; the eminent divine to whom we allude was deputed to examine them, and the first question he put to each was, "Can you boil a potato?"—*Quarterly Review.*

BOILED MUTTON.

A farmer, Charles Lamb's chance companion in a coach, kept boring him to death with questions as to the state of the crops. At length he put a poser—"And pray, sir, how are turnips t'year?" "Why, that, sir, (stammered out Lamb,) will depend upon the boiled legs of mutton."

RISE AND FALL OF KINGDOMS.

Middleton, in his Life of Cicero, speaking of the opinion entertained of Britain by that orator and his contemporary Romans, has the following passage: "From their railleries of this kind, on the barbarity and misery of our island, one cannot help reflecting on the surprising fate and revolutions of kingdoms; how Rome, once the mistress of the world, the seat of arts, empire, and glory, now lies sunk in sloth, ignorance, and poverty, enslaved to the most cruel, as well as to the most contemptible of tyrants, superstition and religious imposture: while this remote country, anciently the jest and contempt of the polite Romans, is become the happy seat of liberty, plenty, and letters; flourishing in all the arts and refinements of civil life; yet running, perhaps, the same course which Rome itself had run before it, from virtuous industry to wealth; from wealth to luxury; from luxury to an impatience of discipline and corruption of morals; till by a total degeneracy and loss of virtue, being grown ripe for destruction, it falls a prey at last to some hardy oppressor, and with the loss of liberty, losing every thing that is valuable, sinks gradually again into its original barbarism."

RED-HAIRED MEN.

Sydney Smith, alluding to the foolishness of excluding Catholics from Parliament, says: "I have often thought if the *wisdom of our ancestors* had excluded all persons with red hair from the House of Commons, of the throes and convulsions it would occasion to restore them to their natural rights. What mobs and riots would it produce? To what infinite abuse and obloquy would the capillary patriot be exposed? what wormwood would distil from one politician? what froth would drop from another? how one lord would work away about the hair of King William and Lord Somers, and the authors of the great and glorious Revolution? how another* would appeal to the Deity and his own virtues, and to the hair of his children? Some would say that red-haired men were superstitious; some would prove they were atheists; they would be petitioned against as the friends of slavery, and the advocates for revolt;

* Lord Eldon, celebrated for his lachrymal qualities, and for "appealing to his own virtues" in his speeches.

in short, such a corrupter of the heart and the understanding is the spirit of persecution, that these unfortunate people, (conspired against by their fellow-subjects of every complexion,) if they did not emigrate to countries where hair of another colour was persecuted, would be driven to the falsehood of perukes, or the hypocrisy of the Tricosian fluid."

A GOOD DINNER.

"A good soup," said the late Earl of Dudley, "a small turbot, a neck of venison, ducklings with green peas, or chicken with asparagus, and an apricot tart, is a dinner for an emperor—when he cannot get a better."

LIFE'S SECOND MORNING.

There are not many more beautiful lines in the English language, there are certainly none so beautiful in the writings of their author, as those of Mrs. Barbauld, which the poet Rogers is fond of repeating to his friends, in his fine, deliberate manner, with just enough of tremulousness in that grave voice of his, to give his recitation the effect of deep feeling.

"Life! we've been long together,
Through pleasant and through cloudy weather.
'Tis hard to part when friends are dear,
Perhaps 'twill cost a sigh, a tear.
Then steal away, give little warning,
Choose thine own time;
Say not good night, but, in some happier clime,
Bid me good morning."

It makes the thought of Death cheerful to represent it thus, as Life looking in upon you with a glad greeting, amidst fresh airs and glorious light. The lines I infer were written by Mrs. Barbauld in her late old age, and I do not wonder that the aged poet, who some years since entered upon the fifth score of his years, should find them haunting his memory.—*Bryant.*

EDUCATION.

There is a tendency in modern education to cover the fingers with rings, and at the same time to cut the sinews at the wrist.

The worst education, which teaches self-denial, is better than the best which teaches every thing else, and not that.—*Sterling.*

CURRAN.

As an example of powerful unpremeditated eloquence, may be given a short answer of Curran, the Irish orator, to a certain Judge Robinson—"the author of many stupid, slavish, and scurrilous political pamphlets," and by his demerits and servility raised to the eminence which he thus disgraced—who, upon one occasion, when the barrister was arguing a case before him, had the brutality to reproach Curran with his poverty, by telling him that he suspected "his law library was rather contracted."

"It is true, my lord," said Curran, with dignified respect, "that I am poor, and the circumstance has certainly somewhat curtailed my library: my books are not numerous, but they are select, and I hope they have been perused with proper dispositions. I have prepared myself for this high profession rather by the study of a few good works, than by the composition of a great many bad ones. I am not ashamed of my poverty; but I should be ashamed of my wealth, could I have stooped to acquire it, by servility and corruption. If I rise not to rank, I shall at least be honest; and should I ever cease to be so, many an example shows me that an ill-gained reputation, by making me the more conspicuous, would only make me the more universally and the more notoriously contemptible!"

FEMALE EDUCATION.

The pursuit of knowledge is the most innocent and interesting occupation which can be given to the female sex; nor can there be a better method of checking a spirit of dissipation than by diffusing a taste for literature. *The true way to attack vice, is by setting up something else against it.* Give to women, in early youth, something to acquire, of sufficient interest and importance to command the application of their mature faculties, and to excite their perseverance in future life; teach them that happiness is to be derived from the acquisition of knowledge, as well as the gratification of vanity; and you will raise up a much more formidable barrier against dissipation than a host of invectives and exhortations can supply.—*Sydney Smith.*

EDUCATION AT BOTANY BAY.

Sydney Smith, in enforcing the necessity of educating the children of the convicts at Botany Bay, humorously remarks, "Nothing but the earliest attention to the habits of children, can restrain the erratic finger from the contiguous scrip, or prevent the hereditary tendency to larcenous abstraction."

PITT AND WALPOLE.

In a debate, in which Mr. Pitt and some of his young friends had violently attacked old Horace Walpole, the latter complained of the self-sufficiency of the young men of the day, on which Mr. Pitt got up with great warmth, beginning with these words: "With the greatest reverence for the gray hairs of the honourable gentleman—" upon which Walpole pulled off his wig, and showed his head covered with gray hairs, which occasioned a general laughter, in which Pitt joined, and the dispute subsided.

CULTIVATION OF THE MENTAL POWERS.

The age of a cultivated mind is often more complacent, and even more luxurious than the youth. It is the reward of the due use of the endowments bestowed by nature: while they, who in youth have made no provision for age, are left like an unsheltered tree, stripped of its leaves and branches, shaking and withering before the cold blasts of winter. In truth, nothing is so happy to itself and so attractive to others, as a genuine and ripened imagination, that knows its own powers, and throws forth its treasures with frankness and fearlessness. The more it produces, the more capable it becomes of production; the creative faculty grows by indulgence; and the more it combines, the more means and varieties of combinations it discovers.—*Sir Egerton Brydges.*

GOOD RULE.

One of the wisest rules that can be observed in study, is to eschew those subjects which afford no footing to the mind.—*St. John.*

ACCESSION TO THE THRONE.

A traveller, benighted in a wild and mountainous country, at length beheld the welcome light of a neighbouring habitation. He urged his horse towards it, when, instead of a house, he approached a kind of illuminated chapel, from whence issued the most alarming sounds he had ever heard. Though greatly surprised and terrified, he ventured to look through a window of the building, when he was amazed to see a large assembly of cats, who, arranged in solemn order, were lamenting over the corpse of one of their own species, which lay in state, and was surrounded with the various emblems of sovereignty. Alarmed and terrified at this extraordinary spectacle, he hastened from the place with greater eagerness than he approached it, and arriving some time after at the house of a gentleman, who never turned the wanderer from his gate, the impressions of what he had seen were so visible on his countenance, that his friendly host inquired into the cause of his anxiety. He accordingly told him his story, and having finished it, a large family cat, who had lain during the narrative before the fire, immediately started up, and very articulately exclaimed, "*Then I am King of the Cats!*" and having thus announced his new dignity, the animal darted up the chimney, and was seen no more.—*Lord Lyttleton's Letters.*

SHERIDAN'S WIT.

Sheridan's wit was eminently brilliant, and almost always successful; it was like all his speaking, exceedingly well prepared, but it was skillfully introduced and happily applied; and it was well mingled also with humour, occasionally descending to farce. How little it was the inspiration of the moment, all men were aware who knew his habits; and in the secret note-books of this famous wit, we are enabled to trace the jokes in embryo, with which he had so often made the walls of St. Stephen's shake, in a merriment excited by the happy appearance of a sudden unpremeditated effusion.

Take an instance in an extract from Sheridan's common-place book: "He employs his fancy in his narrative, and keeps his recollections for his wit." The same idea is expanded into, "When he makes his jokes you applaud the accuracy of his memory, and 'tis only when he states his facts that you admire the flights of his imagination." But the thought was too good to be thus wasted on the desert air of a common-place book. So it came forth at the expense of Kelly, who, having been a composer of music, became a wine merchant. "You will," said the ready wit, "import your music, and compose your wine." Nor was this service exacted from an old idea thought sufficient: so in the House of Commons, an easy, and apparently off-hand parenthesis was thus filled with it, at the cost of Mr. Dundas: "(who generally resorts to his memory for his jokes, and to his imagination for his facts.)"—*Brougham.*

OATS IN SCOTLAND.

Lord Elibank made a happy retort on Dr. Johnson's definition of oats: "a grain, which in England is generally given to the horses, but in Scotland supports the people." "Yes," said he, "and where else will you see *such horses* and *such men?*"

DR. JOHNSON'S CLUB-ROOM.

The club-room is before us, and the table on which stands the omelet for Nugent, and the lemons for Johnson. There are assembled those heads which live for ever on the canvas of Reynolds. There are the spectacles of Burke, and the tall thin form of Langton; the courtly sneer of Beauclerc, and the beaming smile of Garrick; Gibbon rapping his snuff-box, and Sir Joshua with his trumpet in his ear. In the foreground is that strange figure, which is as familiar to us as the figures of those among whom we have been brought up—the gigantic body, the huge massy face, seamed with scars of disease; the brown coat, the black worsted stockings; the gray wig, with the scorched foretop; the dirty hands, the nails bitten and pared to the quick. We see the eyes and nose moving with convulsive twitches; we see the heavy form rolling; we hear it puffing; and then comes the "Why, sir?" and the "What then, sir?" and the "No, sir!" and the "You don't see your way through the question, sir!"—*Macaulay.*

INVITATION TO DINNER.

The following, one of the latest unpublished productions of the poet Moore, addressed to the Marquis of Lansdowne, shows, that though by this time inclining to threescore and ten, he retains all the fire and vivacity of early youth. It is full of those exquisitely apt allusions and felicitous turns of expression in which the English Anacreon excels. It breathes the very spirit of classic festivity. Such an invitation to dinner, is enough to create an appetite in any lover of poetry:

"Some think we bards have nothing real—
  That poets live among the stars, so
Their very dinners are ideal,—
  (And heaven knows, too oft they are so:)
For instance, that we have, instead
  Of vulgar chops and stews and hashes,
First course,—a phœnix at the head,
  Done in its own celestial ashes;
At foot, a cygnet, which kept singing
All the time its neck was wringing.

Side dishes, thus,—Minerva's owl,
Or any such like learned fowl;
Doves, such as heaven's poulterer gets
When Cupid shoots his mother's pets.
Larks stew'd in morning's roseate breath,
  Or roasted by a sunbeam's splendour;
And nightingales, be-rhymed to death—
  Like young pigs whipp'd to make them tender.
Such fare may suit those bards who're able
To banquet at Duke Humphrey's table;
But as for me, who've long been taught
  To eat and drink like other people,
And can put up with mutton, bought
  Where Bromham rears its ancient steeple,
If Lansdowne will consent to share
My humble feast, though rude the fare,
Yet, seasoned by that salt he brings
From Attica's salinest springs,
'Twill turn to dainties; while the cup,
Beneath his influence brightening up,
Like that of Baucis, touched by Jove,
Will sparkle fit for gods above!"

MATHEMATICAL SAILORS.

Nathaniel Bowditch, the translator of Laplace's *Mécanique Céleste*, displayed in very early life a taste for mathematical studies. In the year 1788, when he was only fifteen years old, he actually made an almanac for the year 1790, containing all the usual tables, calculations of the eclipses and other phenomena, and even the customary predictions of the weather.

Bowditch was bred to the sea, and in his early voyages taught navigation to the common sailors about him. Captain Prince, with whom he often sailed, relates, that one day the supercargo of the vessel said to him, "Come, captain, let us go forward, and hear what the sailors are talking about, under the lee of the long-boat." They went forward accordingly, and the captain was surprised to find the sailors, instead of spinning their long yarns, earnestly engaged with book, slate, and pencil, discussing the high matters of tangents and secants, altitudes, dip, and refraction. Two of them, in particular, were very zealously disputing,—one of them calling out to the other, "Well, Jack, what have you got?" I've got the *sine*," was the answer. "But that ain't right," said the other; "*I* say it is the *cosine.*"

DILATORY INCLINATIONS.

Sir Robert Peel, speaking of Lord Eldon, remarked, that "even his failings leaned to virtue's side;" upon which it was observed, that his lordship's failings resembled the leaning tower of Pisa, which, in spite of its long inclination, had never yet *gone over.*

TURNER—RETALIATION.

Campbell relates:—"Turner, the painter, is a ready wit. Once, at a dinner, where several artists, amateurs, and literary men were convened, a poet, by way of being facetious, proposed as a toast, the health of the *painters* and *glaziers* of Great Britain. The toast was drank; and Turner, after returning thanks for it, proposed the health of the British *paper-stainers.*"

DANGEROUS FOOLS.

If men are to be fools, it were better that they were fools in little matters than in great; dullness, turned up with temerity, is a livery all the worse for the facings; and the most tremendous of all things is a magnanimous dunce.—*Sydney Smith.*

HORNE TOOKE AND WILKES.

Horne Tooke having challenged Wilkes, then sheriff of London and Middlesex, received the following reply: "Sir, I do not think it my business to cut the throat of every desperado that may be tired of his life, but as I am at present High Sheriff of the city of London, it may happen that I shall shortly have an opportunity of attending you in my official capacity, in which case I will answer for it, that you shall have *no ground* to complain of my endeavours to serve you."

FOOTE'S WOODEN LEG.

There is no Shakspeare or Roscius upon record, who, like Foote, supported a theatre for a series of years by his own acting, in his own writings; and for ten years of the time upon a wooden leg! This prop to his person I once saw standing by his bedside, ready dressed in a handsome silk stocking, with a polished shoe and gold buckle, awaiting the owner's getting up; it had a kind of tragic, comical appearance, and I leave to inveterate wags the ingenuity of punning upon a Foote in bed, and a leg out of it. The proxy for a limb thus decorated, though ludicrous, is too strong a reminder of amputation, to be very laughable. His undressed supporter was the common wooden stick, which was not a little injurious to a well-kept pleasure-ground. I remember following him after a shower of rain, upon a nicely rolled terrace, in which he stumped a deep round hole at every other step he took, till it appeared as if the gardener had been there with his dibble, preparing, against all horticultural practice, to plant a long row of cabbages in a gravel walk.—*George Colman.*

SIR JOSHUA REYNOLD'S DINNERS.

Sir Joshua Reynolds appears to have been but an irregular manager in his conviviality. "Often," says Forster, "was the dinner-board, prepared for seven or eight, required to accommodate itself to fifteen or sixteen; for often, on the very eve of dinner, would Sir Joshua tempt afternoon visitors with intimation that Johnson, or Garrick, or Goldsmith was to dine there. Nor was the want of seats the only difficulty. A want of knives and forks, of plates and glasses, as often succeeded. In something of the same style too, was the attendance; the kitchen had to keep pace with the visitors, and it was easy to know the guests best acquainted with the house, by their never failing to call instantly for beer, bread, or wine, that they might get them before the first course was over, and the worst confusion began. Once was Sir Joshua prevailed upon to furnish his table with dinner-glasses and decanters, and some saving of time they proved; yet, as they were demolished in the course of service, he could never be prevailed upon to replace them." "But these trifling embarrassments," says Mr. Courtenay, describing them to Sir James Mackintosh; "only served to enhance the hilarity and the singular pleasure of the entertainment. It was not the wine, dishes, and cookery; not the fish and venison that were talked of or recommended; those social hours, that irregular convivial talk, had matter of higher relish, and far more eagerly enjoyed. And amid all the animated bustle of his guests, the host sat perfectly composed; always attentive to what was said, never minding what was ate or drank, and leaving every one at perfect liberty to scramble for himself."—*Life of Goldsmith.*

DOMESTIC HAPPINESS.

Nothing hinders the constant agreement of people who live together, but mere vanity; a secret insisting upon what they think their dignity or merit, and inward expectation of such an over-measure of deference and regard, as answers to their own extravagant false scale, and which nobody can pay, because none but themselves can tell readily to what pitch it amounts.—*Pope.*

LORD BATHURST.

This peer died at the age of 91. Till within a month of his death, he constantly rode out two hours in the morning, and drank his bottle of wine after dinner. Upon one occasion he invited a large party to meet his son, who had become Lord Chancellor, when the whole company sat late except the latter, who took his leave at the decorous hour of twelve. "Come," said the aged earl, "now the *old gentleman* is gone, we can manage to take another bottle."

TRANSFORMATIONS.

Some would trace the pope himself, with his triple crown on his head, and the keys of heaven and hell in his pocket, to our old acquaintance Cerberus, with his three heads, who kept guard as the custos of Tartarus and Elysium.

Be this as it may—the pun of Swift is completely realized. The very same piece, which the Romans adored, now, with a new head on its shoulders—like an old friend with a new face—is worshipped with equal devotion by the modern Italians; and Jupiter appears again, with as little change of name as of materials, in the character of the *Jew*, *Peter*. And, as if they wished to make the resemblance as perfect as possible, they have, in imitation of the

Centum aras posuit, vigilemque, sacraverat ignem

of his pagan prototype, surrounded the tomb of the Apostle with a hundred ever-burning lights. It is really surprising to see with what apparent fervour of devotion, all ranks, and ages, and sexes, kneel to, and kiss the toe of this brazen image; for there is certainly nothing in the "christened Jove" of St. Peter's, as a piece of sculpture, to palliate the superstition of its votaries. They rub it against their lips, with the most reverential piety. I have sat by the hour to see the crowds of people, who flock in to perform this ceremony, waiting for their turn to kiss; and yet the catholic would laugh at the pious Mussulman, who performs a pilgrimage to Mecca, to wash the holy pavement and kiss the black stone of the Caaba—which, like his own St. Peter, is also a relic of heathenism. Alas, poor human nature! The catholic laughs at the Mussulman—we do not scruple to laugh at the catholic—the deist laughs at us—and the atheist laughs at all. What is truth? We must wait for an answer. But though all must *wait the great teacher—Death*, to decide between them, let *us* repose our hopes and fears, with humble confidence, in the promises of Christianity; not as it appears disfigured and disguised at Rome, but as it is written and recorded in that sacred volume, which, in the words of Locke, has "God for its author, salvation for its end, and *truth* without any mixture of error for its matter."—*Matthews.*

Contents.

www.ingramcontent.com/pod-product-compliance
Lightning Source LLC
LaVergne TN
LVHW011223110826
845150LV00006B/1528

* 9 7 8 1 4 2 5 5 1 5 8 0 5 *